THE CHILD'S BOOK ON THE SABBATH

THE CHILD'S BOOK ON THE SABBATH

HORACE HOOKER

Solid Ground Christian Books
Birmingham, Alabama USA

Solid Ground Christian Books
2090 Columbiana Rd, Suite 2000
Birmingham, AL 35216
205-443-0311
sgcb@charter.net
http://solid-ground-books.com

The Child's Book on the Sabbath

Horace Hooker (1794-1865)

Taken from 1835 edition by American Tract Society, New York

Solid Ground Classic Reprints

First printing of new edition April 2006

Cover work by Borgo Design, Tuscaloosa, AL
Contact them at nelbrown@comcast.net

Cover image is titled *Distributing the Blessed Bread*, which was engraved by A.B. Cross.

ISBN: 1-59925-063-2

PREFACE.

The children and youth of the present generation will, without doubt, have to decide whether the Sabbath shall be preserved to our country, as a day holy to the Lord. Ought they not, then, to know the nature and value of this institution, and the dangers which threaten its existence? However others may feel, the author must regard this subject as one respecting which the young ought to be faithfully and fully instructed. If, with a fair view of the design of the Sabbath; of the authority by which it is established; and of its close connection with the interests and eternal destinies of men, the youth of our country shall say, " Let the Sabbath cease to be holy, let it be a day of dissipation and merriment," we should weep over their decision. But, having set before them their duty, we should still have the satisfaction of feeling that we have done what we could to prevent this calamitous result.

It has been the design of the author, in the following pages, to employ such language and modes of illustration, as shall render the subject not only intelligible, but interesting to the young. At the same time, he has kept in view persons of more advanced age; and he indulges the hope that what he has written may not be unprofitable to readers of this class.

Some may think that so much notice ought not o have been taken of objections against the Sabbath, lest it should weaken respect for the institution. If the young could be kept in ignorance of these objections, the author would assent to this view of the subject. But, at the present day, such a thing cannot reasonably be expected. The enemies of the Sabbath are many, and they are active and bitter in their opposition. Tracts, and pamphlets, and newspapers, and all the means of disseminating truth are now perverted to the diffusion of error. It is impossible to prevent this. Shall the advocates of the Sabbath, then, state the objections of the enemy fairly, and refute them by clear and convincing arguments,—or shall they suffer them to be brought before the minds of the young, when no one is at hand to show their fallacy? The former course seems most expedient to the author.

It is suggested, whether parents might not profitably make a chapter of this book the ground-work of a short exercise with their children on the Sabbath. A succession of such exercises, until all the chapters had passed under review, would revive in their own minds the reasons in favor of the Sabbath, and impress these reasons on the minds of their children. A similar exercise, perhaps, might not be unsuitable for classes in Sabbath-schools.

CONTENTS.

EVENING I.

SABBATH SET APART IN PARADISE.

Mrs. Martyn. Why Mrs. M. had these conversations with her children. Why God rested on the seventh day, sanctifying the Sabbath. Sabbath, why sanctified. Reason universal. Sabbath by anticipation. Illustration of it. Answer to the objection. God kind in giving us the Sabbath.   11

EVENING II.

SABBATH SET APART IN PARADISE.

Not mentioned until the time of Moses. Illustration from History of Charles V. Mosaic account brief. Not mentioned for almost five hundred years after Joshua. Early division of time into weeks. Probably on account of the Sabbath. Ancient heathen had a Sabbath. Objections from 16th chapter of Exodus. Answer. Case supposed. Good men love the Sabbath. Sabbath needed by all. Probably kept by Noah, Abraham, and Jacob. Review.   23

EVENING III.

SABBATH DESIGNED FOR ALL.

Page.

Fourth commandment. Not designed only for the Jews. Nor a part of the ceremonial law. Jewish punishment of Sabbath-breaking. Not binding on us. Explanation of moral commandments. Positive commandments. Difference between ceremonial and moral law. Illustrations. Ten things spoken by God to Israel. Sabbath among them. Sabbath a memorial of creation. Occupies a peculiar place. Written by the Holy Spirit on the heart. Recapitulation. 38

EVENING IV.

SABBATH DESIGNED FOR ALL.

The boy that broke the Sabbath, and was hurt. Accidents on the Sabbath. Special judgments. Sabbath, sign of the covenant. Answer. The Nile. The rainbow. Fourth commandment has not expired of its own limitation. Illustration from law of Congress. Not repealed. Objection from Paul's writings examined. Prophets predicted the continuance of the Sabbath. Sabbath as necessary for Christians as for Jews, and more important. 51

EVENING V.

CHANGE OF THE SABBATH.

Time divided into three periods. Some great event commemorated by each. A change to be expected when Christ came. Proofs of a change from the Bible. No express command for the change. Reason. Testimony of early writers. Ignatius. Pliny. Justin Martyr. Eusebius. The change is consistent with the fourth commandment. Supposed case. Jews in Palestine. Sandwich Islands. Sailing round the world in different directions changes the day of the Sabbath. 68

EVENING VI.

SABBATH NECESSARY FOR THE BODY.

Things fitted to each other. Examples. Sabbath fitted to man. Sabbath necessary for the body. Examples. Statement of H. R. Schoolcraft. Of Dr. Spurzheim. Of Dr. Rush. Of Dr. Farre. Animals and vegetables do not need the Sabbath. Sabbath a blessing to the poor. Price of labor. As much for six days' work as for seven. 81

EVENING VII.

SABBATH NECESSARY FOR THE MIND.

Mind needs rest. Anecdote of Sir Isaac Newton. Brain the organ of thought. Influence of long-continued feeling. Case of Mrs. F. Sabbath diverts and soothes the mind. Marquis of Londonderry. Mr. Wilberforce. Sabbath aids the judgment. Illustration. Sabbath fitted to man's moral nature. Hymn. 98

EVENING VIII.

SABBATH NECESSARY FOR SOCIETY.

Laws enforcing the Sabbath. Promotes the welfare of society. Objection, that the Sabbath increases dissipation. Answer. Influence of a day of repose on good morals. "Truce of God" described. Sabbath promotes intelligence. Illustration. Deacon Stockton and father of Thomas Bradish. Sabbath a common school. 111

EVENING IX.

SABBATH NECESSARY FOR SOCIETY.

Influence of Sabbath-schools. Dr. Milne. Books for the Sabbath. Sabbath aids in governing men. Illustrations. Men not governed by laws only. Nor by force only. Case of France. Sabbath peculiarly necessary in a Republic. New England. France. Spain. Scotland in 1763 and in 1783. Proportion of criminals that break the Sabbath. Boy in State Prison. Remark of Baxter. Sabbath in United States more valuable than in other countries. 122

EVENING X.

MANNER OF KEEPING THE SABBATH.

What is meant by remembering the Sabbath. Rest of the Sabbath, not idleness. Necessary repose may be taken. Late labor on Saturday evening. Public worship a duty on the Sabbath. Required of the Jews. Delightful to good men of old. Neglect of, sign of declension. Promotes humility. Preparation for public worship. Children at play in the house of God. Sleeping during public worship. Examples. Farmer Hughes. Mr. Dickman, the blacksmith. Mr. Mortimer, the merchant. Talking politics. Robbing orchards during intermission. 134

EVENING XI.

MANNER OF KEEPING THE SABBATH.

Page.

Private devotion, reading and meditation. Criticism on sermon. Conversation about dress. Variety of exercises prevents fatigue. Example of Judge P. Family instruction on the Sabbath. Men divided into families in Eden. Fourth, a family commandment. Close of the Sabbath. A recollection. Places where children can enjoy the Sabbath. Domestics have a right to the Sabbath. Beasts of labor have a right to rest. Anecdote. Heart in the duties of the Sabbath. 149

EVENING XII.

VIOLATIONS OF THE SABBATH.

Some things may be done on the Sabbath. Rules to decide what. Illustration from the small pox. Case of danger of losing a debt. Of sailing in a steamboat. Of labor when a crop is in danger. Jews forbidden to labor in harvest. Poverty no excuse. We ought not to let a crop spoil. Answer. Crop saved from fire. Reasons for the difference. Improper conversation. Sinful thoughts. How to judge on this subject. Wrong to go to the Post Office. Exception. Or to travel. Or to work for a living. The stage-driver. Government no right to violate the Sabbath. Rule respecting labor. 160

EVENING XIII.

MOTIVES FOR KEEPING THE SABBATH.

Page.

The command of God. Our own good. God's promise. What it has done for our country. The safety of our country. Others indisposed to keep the Sabbath. If not well kept, will be a curse. Example and testimony of good men. Nehemiah. Sir Matthew Hale's testimony. Dr. Johnson and Sir Joshua Reynolds. Bishop Porteus and Prince of Wales. Increases one's influence. Sign of our reverence for God. Mr. Wilberforce and Mrs. Hannah More. Moving power of the moral world. Illustration. Different ends of a well kept, and an abused Sabbath. 176

EVENING XIV.

DANGERS THREATENING THE SABBATH.

Transportation of the mail. Growth and influence of large cities. Increase of manufacturing villages. Of luxury and wealth. Of want of religious instruction. Unfavorable circumstances of new settlements. Dislike of religious restraint. Growing laxness among good men. Change in mode of keeping the Sabbath. Facts. Increase of Roman Catholics. Sabbath in Paris and Malta. Cathedral dedicated in St. Louis. What can the young do for the Sabbath? Must give up all else sooner than the Sabbath. 190

THE CHILD'S BOOK
ON THE SABBATH.

EVENING I.

SABBATH SET APART IN PARADISE.

George, Charles, and Susan, are the names of the children who will be frequently mentioned in what I am now about to write. George was thirteen, Charles eleven, and Susan nearly nine years of age. If any of my young readers doubt whether there ever were two such boys as George and Charles, and such a little girl as Susan; they may suppose that some other children with these names said what I represent George, and Charles, and Susan as saying in this story. Perhaps you may think there never was such a person as the woman I call Mrs. Martyn, the mother of these little children; well, then, you may suppose, if you please, that your own mother says to you what I represent Mrs. Martyn as saying to her children.

The husband of Mrs. Martyn was a physician. He was obliged to be absent from his family a good deal, and that was the reason why Mrs. Martyn took the chief charge of their education. She was a woman of good sense, and she had studied more than most women, because she wished to know how to teach her children. It is a great blessing to have a pious and sensible mother, who can instruct her children about God, and their own souls, and the way to be happy hereafter.

Mrs. Martyn used, every Sabbath evening, to call her children around her, and ask them what they remembered about the texts and the sermons which they had heard that day. And sometimes she would tell them a story out of the Bible, or read to them some useful book, which she thought would instruct them and make them better.

I have known some fathers and mothers who made their children repeat the catechism to them on Sabbath evening, but the children did not love at all to have the time come for saying the catechism. George, and Charles, and Susan Martyn, however, always loved to gather around their mother after supper on the Sabbath—for it made them happy to see their mother so pleasant and cheerful. Mrs. Martyn always tried to be cheerful, and especially on the Sabbath, and when she talked with her children on serious subjects. She thought that if she was gloomy, her children might think religion made her so, and they would not wish to be religious. I believe there are few children who would not, on Sabbath evening, love to sit on the knees of their parents, or to stand by their side, and say the catechism,—but would think it the happiest time in the week,—if their parents only looked a little more cheerful and pleasant.

Mrs. Martyn had often talked with her children about the Sabbath, and had taught them to keep it holy. She began to think, however, that it was time to tell them, more particularly, why they ought to love and observe the Sabbath. She wished to have them able, when they grew up, to give to others a reason for resting on the Sabbath, and for keeping their thoughts from worldly business. She knew that if they lived, they would be tempted to break the Sabbath, and that while they were young was the best time to guard them against these temptations.

She had another reason for wishing them to be instructed, now, about the Sabbath. A brother of Dr. Martyn lived near by, and often visited the family. He did not care at all for the Sabbath. To be sure, he did not work on that day, because it would grieve his friends, and because others would talk about it. But he would often speak disrespectfully concerning the Sabbath before her children.

Mrs. Martyn thought George was old enough to understand all the reasons for keeping the Sabbath, and that Charles and Susan, if they could not understand all the reasons, might understand enough to do them much good.

She waited several weeks, hoping that her husband might be able to give them some lessons about keeping the Sabbath. But he was too busy in curing the sick. So she determined to wait no longer. She began to read all the good books she could find on the subject. She thought it all over herself, and when she was prepared, she told George, and Charles, and Susan, after tea one Sabbath evening, that she wished them to be very attentive to what she should say to them about the Sabbath. She told them that she hoped they would never forget it, but remember it when their mother was lying in the grave, and could not talk with them, and give them good advice any more.

Mrs. Martyn's voice trembled, and a tear stood in her eye, as she thought how soon she might be torn from her dear children. But she wiped away the tear, and in a moment was as cheerful as ever. The thought only made her spirit a little more serious, and her silent prayer more earnest, that she might say something which would do her children good, and fit them for the endless Sabbath. George, and Charles, and Susan were very sad at what their mother told them, and said, they hoped their mother would live as long as they did.

The sun cast his mellow evening rays into the windows of the room where Mrs. Martyn and her children sat around a table, on which were a large Bible, a hymn book, and several other serious books, which they had been reading. Mrs. Martyn began her conversation about the Sabbath.

Mrs. M. George, can you tell me how long it is since the world was created?

George. Almost six thousand years, mother. It was about four thousand years from the creation to the time when our Saviour was born, and it has been more than eighteen hundred years since.

Mrs. M. How long was God in creating the world?

George. Six days, mother.

Mrs. M. Do you suppose, my child, that God could not make the world, though it is so very large, in less than six days?

George. I suppose God could have made this world, and a thousand more worlds just like it, in one day, if he had pleased.

Mrs. M. Why, then, do you think he spent six days in making the world?

George. I think, mother, it must have been because he meant to have men work six days, before they have a day of rest.

Mrs. M. Very well, my son, I think that is the reason.

Now, Charles, see if you can tell me what God did on the seventh day?

Charles. He rested, mother, the Bible tells us— I have read it a great many times.

Susan. Why, mother, did God want to rest? He could not be tired

Mrs. M. Can you answer your little sister's question, Charles?

Charles. Yes, mother, I learned why he rested, in my Sabbath-school lesson.

Mrs. M. Tell Susan, then, what the Bible says about it.

Charles. "And on the seventh day God ended his work which he made; and he rested on the seventh day from all his work which he had made. And God blessed the seventh day, and sanctified it; because that in it he had rested from all his work which God created and made."

Mrs. M. I am glad, my son, that you remember so well your Sabbath-school lesson. Some children, I fear, forget what they recite on the Sabbath, before the close of the week. But to study so, does very little good.

Susan. What, mother, does it mean, for God to sanctify the Sabbath?

Mrs. M. Come, Charles, you must be Susan's teacher again, I believe.

Charles. Our superintendent, when he asked us questions in the Sabbath-school, said, it means that God has *set apart* the Sabbath for his own use; that he lets men work for themselves six days, but on the Sabbath they must rest from their common work, and spend the day in God's service.

Mrs. M. I feel very thankful that you have so kind and faithful teachers at the Sabbath-school.

SABBATH SET APART IN PARADISE.

You see, then, my children, that it is God who has commanded us to keep the Sabbath; and that he set apart the Sabbath for himself, as soon as he made the world, and before Adam and Eve were driven from the garden of Eden. The Sabbath must be of more consequence to men than almost any thing else, or God would not so soon have commanded them to keep it.

Do you not think it very kind, George, for God to let men eat the flesh of cattle and birds?

George. Yes, mother, I should not know how to live without meat very long.

Mrs. M. Well, my son, I suppose God did not take care that men should have meat to eat, so soon as he took care that they should have the Sabbath.

George. What makes you think so, mother?

Mrs. M. Because the Bible never mentions that men had a right to eat flesh, until after the flood; but it mentions the Sabbath as soon as the world was created.

George. Mother, was the Sabbath meant for every body to keep?

Mrs. M. Certainly. What reason does God give, in the passage which Charles has just repeated, for sanctifying the seventh day as the Sabbath?

George. It was that *he* had rested on the seventh day from all his works.

Mrs. M. What reason is given in the fourth

commandment, why God sanctified the seventh day for the Sabbath?

George. It is the same reason which I have just mentioned. "For in six days the Lord made heaven and earth, the sea and all that in them is, and rested the seventh day; wherefore the Lord blessed the Sabbath day and hallowed it."

Mrs. M. Can you think, my son, of any nation, or of any family, for whose resting this is a better reason, than for any others' resting.

George. No, mother, I cannot see why God's resting on the seventh day, is any more reason why the Jews should rest than why we should rest.

Mrs. M. It is no more reason, my child. But what made you ask if it was meant that every body should keep the Sabbath?

George. Uncle John said the other day, that he was not going to keep the Sabbath; for God did not command any body to keep it, except the Jews.

Mrs. M. I am sorry, my son, that your uncle John says so. You must not mind what he tells you about such things, if it contradicts what the Bible says.

George. But, mother, uncle John said that God did not command men to keep the Sabbath, until long after the world was created. He said that Moses mentioned the sanctification of the Sabbath, by anticipation. I do not think I understand what he meant; can you tell me, mother?

Mrs. M. I will try to explain it to you. Suppose I were to tell you the history of New England. I should very soon get down to the year 1620, when the first white settlers, who are called, sometimes, pilgrim fathers, came to this country. I should then describe how, one cold day in December, they landed on Plymouth Rock. I might then say, wherefore the sons of the pilgrims come together, every year, at Plymouth, and celebrate the twenty-second of December as a festival, because on that day their ancestors landed on Plymouth Rock.

It was, I think, about two hundred years after the landing of the pilgrims, before their sons began to celebrate the twenty-second of December. But in my story, I join together the landing of the pilgrims, and the celebration of their landing, though one was almost two hundred years before the other. Your uncle John thinks Moses does just so in his account of the creation. He thinks that Moses joins together God's resting on the seventh day, and the setting apart of that day for the Sabbath, though the seventh day was not set apart for the service of God until twenty-five hundred years after God rested from the work of creation. And this is what your uncle John meant, when he told you that Moses, in his history mentions the Sabbath by anticipation.

George. I think I understand it, now, mother; but is what uncle John says about this true?

Mrs. M. I do not think it is true.

George. Why do you not think it is true?

Mrs. M. Do you remember what God did, on the different days in which he made the world?

Charles. I remember, mother.

Mrs. M. Well, then, you may tell us.

Charles. On the first day God made the light. On the second day he made the firmament. On the third day he made the dry land. On the fourth day he told the sun and moon to shine. On the fifth day he told the fish to swim about in the sea, and the fowls to fly up high in the air. On the sixth day he made the oxen and elephants, and all the beasts and creeping things. And I suppose, that towards the close of the day he made Adam.

Mrs. M. Very well, Charles, but what did God do on the seventh day?

Charles. God rested on the seventh day and sanctified it for the Sabbath.

Mrs. M. Moses says so, my children. He tells what God did on the seventh day, just as he tells what God did on the sixth day, and on the fifth day, and on the other days.

Do you think, George, that what Moses represents God as doing on the fourth day, was not done until two thousand five hundred years afterwards?

SABBATH SET APART IN PARADISE.

George. No, mother, I suppose the sun and moon were made on the fourth day, just as Moses says they were.

Mrs. M. But you might just as well affirm that the sun and moon were not made until two thousand five hundred years after Moses declares they were made, as that God did not sanctify the Sabbath on the seventh day.

George. I think, mother, of another reason for believing that the Sabbath was sanctified at the close of creation. The Bible says in the fourth commandment: "For in six days the Lord made heaven and earth, the sea and all that in them is, and rested the seventh day; wherefore the Lord blessed the Sabbath day, and hallowed it." Now, mother, the Bible does not say, here, "wherefore the Lord *blesses* the Sabbath day." Nor does it say, wherefore the Lord *will bless* the Sabbath day; it says, that God had *already* "*blessed* the Sabbath day and hallowed it," before he spoke to the Israelites from Sinai—and when was this done, if not when he rested from his work on the seventh day?

Mrs. M. It is as you say, my son, and I am glad to see that you have thought so much on the subject.

George. I think it would be very strange if the Jews had not been commanded, until they came back from Babylon, to keep the passover, that they might remember how kind God was in passing by their houses while he slew all the first-born of the Egyptians.

Mrs. M. It would have been very strange—but not more strange than that the Sabbath should not have been observed as a memorial of the creation, until the time of Moses, two thousand five hundred years after the world was made.

George. While Adam and Eve were in the garden of Eden, does not the Bible say, " Therefore shall a man leave his father and mother, and shall cleave to his wife; and they twain shall be one flesh ?" Is this, too, said by anticipation ? From the narrative, I should think it quite as likely that Moses got before his story, when he speaks of marriage, as when he speaks of the Sabbath. And from the language of Moses, uncle John, I think, might as well say that marriage was not commanded before the Israelites came out of Egypt, as that men were not commanded to keep the Sabbath before that time.

Mrs. M. We have now talked on the subject enough for one night. Think, my children, how kind God has been to give you the Sabbath. To-day you have been permitted to rest, while a great many little boys and girls have been obliged to work until they were very tired. You have been to church, where good people offered up their prayers and praises to God. You have heard the invitations of mercy, and been told what you must do to be saved. Accept these invitations—obey these words, do not forget them, for, one day, the Lord Jesus Christ will inquire what use you have made of them. And when, before you go to sleep, you thank God for the mercies of another holy day, remember to pray for the many, many children, that know nothing about the Sabbath, and never heard of the Lord Jesus Christ.

EVENING II.

SABBATH SET APART IN PARADISE.

A few minutes after tea, the next Sabbath evening, Mrs. M. went into the room where she had the former conversation with her children about the Sabbath. George, and Charles, and Susan were sitting around the table, waiting for their mother. Mrs. M. told them she was very happy to see so good a sign that they were interested in the subject. The children all said they loved, very much, to converse with their mother respecting the Sabbath, and they hoped that she would talk to them a good while that evening. She asked them if they thought, during the week, of what she had told them in her former conversation.

George. I thought of it, mother, very often, and I want to ask you, now, what makes any body doubt whether God sanctified the Sabbath on the same seventh day on which he rested himself. I read over, last week, again and again, the account which Moses gives of the sanctification of the Sabbath, in Genesis, 2 : 2, 3. I wonder how uncle John, or any body else, can think the seventh day was not sanctified for the Sabbath, at that time.

Mrs. M. The most natural meaning of the language is, that the Sabbath was sanctified at that time. And the reason why your uncle John, and others who agree with him on this point, do not think this is the meaning, is, that they suppose nothing further is said about the Sabbath until the Israelites left Egypt. They think that if Noah, and Abraham, and Jacob had kept the Sabbath, the Bible would have mentioned it.

George. I should think so, too, mother. Does not the Bible say any thing about the Sabbath, from the creation until the time of Moses ?

Mrs. M. The Bible mentions only a few things that happened, for twenty-five hundred years after the world was made. Do you know, George, how many chapters there are in Genesis ?

George. Yes, mother, there are fifty.

Mrs. M. These fifty chapters contain the history

of two thousand three hundred and sixty-nine years, and the first and second chapters of Exodus carry the history down to the time when Moses was keeping the flocks of his father-in-law in Midian. This was two thousand five hundred and thirteen years after the creation. Now, George, how large a book would these fifty chapters of Genesis, and two chapters of Exodus make, if printed just like Robertson's History of Charles V. in your father's library?

George. I do not know, mother—how many pages would they make?

Mrs. M. I have not calculated very accurately I think that if you leave out several chapters which are almost entirely names, and three or four chapters that give an account of the creation of the world, and the fall of man, the remainder would make only about fifty-five pages like those in the History of Charles V. Do you remember, George, how many pages there are in that history?

George. There are five hundred and eighty pages, mother.

Mrs. M. And how old was Charles V. when he died?

George. Fifty-eight years, mother.

Mrs. M. Now, my son, if it takes five hundred and eighty pages to give the history of one man's life, for only fifty-eight years, how very small a part of the history of the whole world, for two thousand five hundred years, can be got into fifty-five or sixty pages?

George. I did not think of that before. I see now that a great many things must be left out, in so brief a history as that of Moses.

Mrs. M. Yes, my son, it must be so. And it would be no wonder if Moses had not mentioned the Sabbath among the few things which he relates in all that long time.

Besides, if you conclude that there was no Sabbath from the creation until the time of Moses, because the Sabbath is not mentioned during this period, you ought to conclude, for the same reason, that there was no Sabbath for almost five hundred years afterward. For the Sabbath is not mentioned in the Bible, from the time of Joshua, to the reign of David. And do you think Joshua and all the good people of Israel forgot the Sabbath, so soon after God came down on Sinai, in flaming fire, and told them to remember the Sabbath-day to keep it holy?

George. No, mother, I think Joshua would love to keep the Sabbath. But is there no evidence that the Sabbath was observed in the world, after God sanctified it, on the seventh day, until the Israelites came out of Egypt?

Mrs. M. The division of time into weeks appears to have been very early. I can see no reason for such a division, unless it marked out the space between one Sabbath and another. The sun and the moon divide time into days, and months, and years —but neither the sun, nor the moon, nor any other heavenly body, divides time into weeks. God told Noah that in *seven* days it should rain on the earth. Again, it is said that after *seven* days, the waters of the flood were upon the earth. Noah, you remember, sent out a dove, to learn whether the waters had dried up. The dove returned. Noah waited *seven* days and sent her out again, and again she returned. After waiting *seven* days more, Noah sent her out again. There was evidently something peculiar about the seventh day, in the time of Noah, and what was it, if not because that day was the Sabbath? In the story of Jacob and Laban, mention is made of the *week*, which shows that time was, at that early period, divided into weeks, and probably so divided on account of the Sabbath.

The ancient heathen respected the seventh day —Homer and Hesiod say that the seventh day was holy. Porphyry, an infidel, says that the Phenicians consecrated one day as holy. Josephus says, that there is no city either of Greeks, or barbarians, or any other nation, where the religion of the Sabbath is not known. All these are ancient writers. Many more ancient writers give the same testimony. But how came the heathen to pay this respect to the seventh day? I have no doubt that they learned from Noah, to regard it as sacred.

George. May they not have been acquainted with the Jewish Sabbath and imitated the Jews?

Mrs. M. I think not, my son. The Jews were hated by some nations, and despised by others, and no nation would have been very likely to imitate them.

George. Uncle John told me, one day last week, that the first account we have that men were ever commanded to keep the Sabbath, is in the sixteenth chapter of Exodus.

Mrs. M. If what I have already told you is to be relied on, my son, this cannot be true. And it seems to me that the sixteenth chapter of Exodus helps to prove the Sabbath was known before the time of Moses.

George. How does it help to prove this, mother?

Mrs. M. After the manna came, the Israelites, on the sixth day, gathered twice as much of it as Moses had commanded them to gather on the other days. Now, why did they do this, if not to provide for the Sabbath?

George. God had informed Moses that on the sixth day there should be twice as much manna gathered as on other days, and Moses may have told the people.

Mrs. M. That cannot be so, I think, for then the rulers must have known as well as the people, what Moses had said, and they would not have gone to tell him what the people had done, as if something unexpected had happened which he did not know, and which required his immediate attention. I conclude, therefore, that the people, without any direction from Moses, gathered twice as much manna on the sixth day, as they had been told to gather on the other days. And I do not see why they should have done this of their own accord, if they did not know that the next day was the Sabbath.

I think, too, the manner in which God speaks to Moses, when he told him that he would give the Israelites manna to eat, shows that Moses was already acquainted with the Sabbath. God said— "And it shall come to pass, that on the sixth day they shall prepare that which they shall bring in; and it shall be twice as much as they gather daily." Now, if Moses before this was ignorant of the Sabbath, I think he would have been apt to inquire why there would be twice as much manna on the sixth day, as on any other day. But he seems not to have been at all surprised, nor to have made any inquiries. The reason, I have no doubt, was, he had always known that the seventh day was the Sabbath, and that on this account a double portion of manna was sent on the sixth day.

The manner in which Moses replied to the rulers, shows that the Sabbath was not known then for the first time. "This is that which the Lord hath said, *To-morrow is the rest of the holy*

Sabbath, unto the Lord your God." But if you will look to the chapter you will see that the Lord had said nothing to Moses about the Sabbath. He had only told Moses that on the sixth day the people must gather twice as much manna as on the other days. But Moses at once infers why this was commanded. So far as appears, he told the people, without God's informing him, that it was because the seventh day is the holy Sabbath. It seems, therefore, that Moses knew of the existence of the Sabbath before God spake to him what is recorded in the sixteenth chapter of Exodus.

Suppose your teacher's father was sick, and he wished to dismiss the school one week, for the sake of visiting him. Do you think he would say, at the close of the school, at night, "To-morrow is the day the vacation begins for a week." Is this the way he would, for the first time, let you know that there was to be a vacation?

George. I think not, mother. I think he would say to us, "My father is sick, and I wish to visit him—there *will be* no school for a week, it *will be* vacation."

Mrs. M. So I think Moses would not have said, "To-morrow *is* the rest of the holy Sabbath unto the Lord," if that was the first time the Israelites had ever heard of the Sabbath. He would have been apt to tell them more about the Sabbath, how they should keep it, and what they should keep it for. And he would have said, "To-morrow *will be* the rest"—not, "To-morrow is the rest."

Mrs. M. I can mention only one or two more reasons for thinking that the Sabbath was observed before the time of Moses. Good men love the Sabbath. They may differ in many other things, but they all agree in this. Now I cannot believe that God deprived Enoch, and Noah, and Abraham, and Isaac, and Jacob, of the privilege of the Sabbath. These men were the friends of God, and the Sabbath would have been their delight. If the Sabbath had been sanctified to commemorate some event which took place after their day, or in which they had no interest, then I could believe that Noah, and Abraham, and Jacob, were never permitted to enjoy the Sabbath. But the reason why God set apart the Sabbath for his own service is, that he rested on the seventh day. This reason, as I told you, in our former conversation, is no more applicable to one man, or to one age, than to another.

The benefits of the Sabbath, too, are needed by all, in every age. Abraham needed the Sabbath for rest as much as Moses. Noah needed the Sabbath for meditation and worshiping God, as much as David. Our Saviour says, the Sabbath was made for man. It is good for men's understandings, for their hearts, and for their bodies, to keep the Sabbath. I cannot believe, therefore, that God let two thousand five hundred years pass, before he sanctified the Sabbath for man.

Susan. Do you think, mother, that Noah kept the Sabbath when he was shut up with the beasts, and birds, and creeping things, in the ark?

Mrs. M. Yes, my dear, I do not doubt that Noah had many a happy Sabbath while the ark was tossing over the flood, and resting on the top of Mount Ararat. And I suppose Enoch, before he was translated to the Sabbath of heaven, spent many a Sabbath on earth, in prayer and praise to God. And when Abraham was living on the plains of Mamre, before Hebron, I think he rested from his labors and cares on the Sabbath. And when Jacob was flying from his brother Esau, and going a long journey into Mesopotamia, I think he would stop in some pleasant grove, and there spend the Sabbath in worship and in meditation.

Now, my dear children, in my former conversation and in this, I have said all I intended to say, to show you that God *instituted the Sabbath and set it apart for his own service*, while Adam and Eve were yet in Paradise. Can you repeat to me, George, the reasons which I have offered to show this?

George. I believe I can remember them all.

Mrs. M. If you cannot, I think Charles or Susan will be able to help you, for they have been very attentive all the evening.

George. The reasons were—Moses says God sanctified the seventh day for the Sabbath, as soon as he had finished making the world. The division of time into weeks seems to have been known in the days of Noah, and it was certainly known in the days of Jacob. This division was, probably, made to mark out the time between one Sabbath and another. The Sabbath, therefore, must have existed then. The manner in which the Sabbath is spoken of in the sixteenth chapter of Exodus, and the gathering of twice as much manna on the sixth day, as on other days, shows that the Sabbath was known before God told the Israelites they must be careful to observe it.

These are all the reasons you gave, are they not, mother?

Charles. I remember two more reasons, mother.

Mrs. M. What are they, my son?

Charles. One was, that good men love to keep the Sabbath; and you could not believe God would deprive Noah, and Abraham, and Jacob of the privilege of keeping it, when God's resting on the seventh day is as good a reason why they should rest, as why the Jews should rest afterwards.

Mrs. M. Very well, Charles: I am glad to find that you have understood me, and can remember so much of what I have said.

Charles. But, mother, I remember another reason;—you said Noah and Abraham needed the Sabbath for resting, and meditating, and worshiping God, as much as Moses and David needed it;

and you could not think that when God made the Sabbath for all mankind, and they all needed it, he would wait two thousand five hundred years after he made the world, before he gave men the Sabbath

Mrs. M. Well, Susan, you see how much your brothers remember of our conversation; have you remembered any of it?

Susan. Yes, mother; I was careful to hear every word, and I understood it almost all, I think, and I remember some of it.

Mrs. M. What do you remember, my dear?

Susan. I remember you said, you suppose Noah kept a good many pleasant Sabbaths when the ark was tossing over the waves, and that Jacob would stop and keep the Sabbath in some pretty grove, when he was flying from his wicked brother Esau.

Mrs. M. How highly, my children, ought we to respect and honor the Sabbath! If it had been established many hundred years ago by a council of the wisest and best men that ever lived, and been honored and observed by good people ever since, it ought not to be lightly disregarded. But when the Sabbath was established by God himself, as soon as he had finished making the world, how much more should we respect and honor it. When we dishonor the Sabbath, we dishonor God, who, by so early sanctifying it, shows how highly he esteems it, and how displeased he must be at its violation.

We ought, also, to set a high value on the Sab

bath, because God not only sanctified, but "*blessed* the seventh day." He so early made it a delightful privilege to keep the Sabbath. He, as it were, gave a pledge, that they who observe it as he commands shall be gainers by their service—that it should be one of the most pleasant and profitable days of the week: and God has, in every age, redeemed his pledge; for all who keep the Sabbath holy enjoy his special presence on that day, and find that its sacred rest fits them not only for the business and trials of this life, but for the everlasting rest of heaven.

And remember, my children, that the Sabbath is *God's day;* he has set it apart from the other days for himself, and told us what he wants us to do on that day in his service. We may work for ourselves on other days, and do what is necessary for our support and comfort. On the Sabbath, if I may so say, we must work for God. If we are idle, and neglect the work which he has told us to do, or attend to other things to which he has forbidden us to attend on that day, he will be angry with us; and if we are not sorry for what we have thus done, and determine to do better in future, he will certainly punish us for it in this world, or in the next.

Were I to tell you that I wish you to study five days every week, but that you may have the sixth day for amusement with your young companions, you would think it very wrong for you to go to the meadows, to gather berries or flowers, on the other days. But it is just as wrong for you to spend the Sabbath in doing any thing which God has forbidden to be done on that day, as to be playing truant when I think you are at school.

And if God has set apart the Sabbath from the other days, none ought to be ashamed to keep and honor it. You would think it very ungrateful, and very wicked, to be ashamed to do something, before your companions, which I had commanded you to do. How much more ungrateful and wicked are those who are ashamed to keep and honor the Sabbath, when in the company of others that ridicule it, and scorn to keep it holy!

Remember too, my children, that they are your enemies, whatever they may pretend, who, by their example or arguments, tempt you to violate the day. God made the Sabbath for man, when he made the earth for man's residence, and filled it with conveniencies and beauties for man to enjoy. It must, therefore, be for man's best good to keep the Sabbath in just the way God has told him to keep it. God knows better than any one else what will make you happy; and he desires, more than any one on earth —more even than your own parents—that you should be happy. No one, therefore, who wishes you to do on the Sabbath what God has said you must not do, can be your friend: he must be your enemy. You would not think a bad boy your friend, who should tempt you, on your way to school, to stop and slide on the ice, when I had told you not to loiter a moment on the road. So you ought always to suspect that those wish to lead you into mischief, who tempt you to do, on the Sabbath, what God has forbidden.

When God thus early sanctified the Sabbath, and blessed it, and when he has always fulfilled his promise to make its observance a privilege, how displeased must he be with those who disregard it, and devote it to their own business or amusement! Thus to misemploy or trifle with the day, is to resist God's authority, despise his blessing, and withhold the service which he has a perfect right to require. No wonder, therefore, he should say, "If ye will not hearken unto me to hallow the Sabbath-day, then will I kindle a fire in your gates, and it shall devour your palaces, and it shall not be quenched."

I have more to tell you about the Sabbath, and I shall be encouraged to go on with our conversation, you all seem to understand and remember it so well.

But it is now time to stop.—We have talked enough for one night. Pray God to keep us through the week, and to let us meet and talk of this subject next Sabbath evening.

EVENING III.

SABBATH BINDING ON ALL.

On the next Sabbath evening, when they had again met around the table, Mrs. Martyn said To-night I mean to show you *that God designed the Sabbath should be observed to the end of the world, and by men of all nations.*

It was chiefly for the sake of proving this that, in our two former conversations, I tried to show you that the Sabbath was instituted by God, or set apart by him for his own service, in the garden of Eden. I need not dwell on this argument. If God sanctified the Sabbath when man was first created, doubtless he meant it not for any particular nation, but for all mankind. Susan, you may repeat the fourth commandment.

Susan. " Remember the Sabbath-day to keep it holy. Six days shalt thou labor and do all thy work; but the seventh day is the Sabbath of the Lord thy God; in it thou shalt not do any work, thou, nor thy son, nor thy daughter, thy man-servant, nor thy maid-servant, nor thy cattle, nor thy stranger that is within thy gates; for in six days the Lord made heaven and earth, the sea and all that in them is, and rested the seventh day; wherefore the Lord blessed the Sabbath-day and hallowed it."

Mrs. M. In this commandment God did not establish any thing new. The Sabbath was given twenty-five hundred years before. But the Jews, when in Egypt, were so very much oppressed, I do not think that their cruel masters would let them rest on the Sabbath. I suppose they had to work as hard on the seventh day, as on any other day of the week, and had almost forgotten the Sabbath. But it was very necessary for them, as it is for all men, that they should keep the Sabbath. So God put the commandment to keep the Sabbath holy, among the commandments in which he shows what he most wishes men should do. You see, therefore, how God values the Sabbath.

George. I am sure nothing is said in the fourth commandment about the Jews, more than about other nations.

Mrs. M. I think there is not, my son. Wherever men have families, or man-servants, or maidservants, or cattle, or visiters, there God commands that the Sabbath should be kept. If none but Jews have such things, then we should suppose none but Jews are included in the fourth commandment.

George. Will you tell me, then, mother, why uncle John says that none but Jews are bound to keep the fourth commandment?

Mrs. M. It is because he supposes that the fourth commandment is one of the ceremonial laws of the Jews, which were done away when our Saviour died.

George. Was the fourth commandment done away then, mother?

Mrs. M. No, my child.—I have shown you that the Sabbath was in existence two thousand five hundred years before the Jewish ceremonial law was given. It existed before that law, and could exist when that law was done away.

George. But uncle John says the Jews punished Sabbath-breaking with death, and that if we think the fourth commandment binding on men now, we must also punish with death those who break the Sabbath.

Mrs. M. Can you tell me, George, how the Jews punished men who were guilty of worshiping graven images?

George. They stoned them to death.

Mrs. M. And how did they punish the man who was profane?

George. They stoned him to death.

Mrs. M. And how did they punish the disobedient child?

George. They stoned him to death.

Mrs. M. Well, George, do you think your uncle John supposes the second, and third, and fifth commandments are parts of the Jewish ceremonial law, and not binding on men at the present day?

George. O no, mother, he said that all the commandments but the fourth were very good, and ought to be kept by every body.

Mrs. M. Why did not you tell him that if we admit the second, third, and fifth commandments to be binding on us as well as on the Jews, then we ought, on this principle, to punish the idolater with death, the profane man with death, and the disobedient child with death?

George. I did not think of it, mother. But if he says again that the fourth commandment was only for the Jews, and is not binding on us, because the Jews punished the Sabbath-breaker with death, I will tell him that for the same reason he must reject the second, and third, and fifth commandments.

Mrs. M. God was the civil Head of the Jewish government. He was King of the Jews, in a different sense from that in which he is King of other nations. He stood in a relation to the Jews similar to that in which an earthly king stands to the country over which he reigns. As civil Ruler, or King of the Jews, God punished the crime of Sabbath-breaking with death. He now punishes Sabbath-breaking as he pleases, and when he pleases, either in this world, or in the next. But he also gives to civil rulers the right to punish Sabbath-breaking as they think proper. He does the same in regard to breaches of the second, third, and fifth commandments. We need not look to see how the Jews punished those guilty of breaking these commandments. We are under no obligation to adopt their mode of punishment. All the way it can interest us is, by showing that God regards the violation of the Sabbath as a heinous sin.

What God added to the original Sabbath, to fit it to the peculiar institutions of the Jews, might cease to exist, and yet the original Sabbath remain in full force. The leaves may fall from the vine that twines around the sturdy oak, and the vine itself die—while the oak may survive its short-lived companion, and battle with the storms of a hundred winters. Just so the Sabbath, which was more than two thousand years old when the Jewish government was formed, may last to the end of time—though that government, with which it was so closely connected, was long ago overthrown.

George. Uncle John said that the other commandments were *moral*, but the fourth commandment was *positive*, and that this is one reason why he thought this commandment was meant only for the Jews. What did he mean, mother, when he said that the other commandments were moral?

Mrs. M. He meant, I suppose, that the other commandments grow out of men's relation to God, and to each other; so that if God had not told us to keep them, we should know they ought to be kept.

George. I do not know that I understand you, mother.

Mrs. M. I will try to explain it. Take the third commandment. If God had not forbidden us to speak his name lightly, or disrespectfully, we should know we ought not to do it. For he is our Maker and Ruler, and then he is so great and good a God, we ought never to speak of him without reverence.

So take the fifth commandment. We should know we ought to obey our father and mother, even if God had not commanded us to do it. Our parents have done so much for us, and suffered so much for us, and we stand in such a relation to them, that our consciences and hearts tell us, without a commandment, that they deserve our love and obedience. This is what I mean when I say that moral commandments grow out of men's relation to God and to each other.

George. And what did uncle John mean when he said that the fourth commandment is only positive?

Mrs. M. I suppose he meant that if God had not commanded us to keep the Sabbath, there is no reason, so far as we can see, why we should be bound to keep it.

Perhaps, after all, you will understand the difference better, between moral and positive commandments, if I were to say, *that* MORAL *commandments are those, the reason for which we can see, and* POSITIVE *commandments those the reason for which we cannot see.*

George. Is there no reason, mother, which we can see for keeping the Sabbath?

Mrs. M. We can see just as much reason for keeping the fourth, as for keeping any other of the commandments. We can see as plainly that rest, one day in seven, tends to preserve the body in health, and the mind and heart in a proper state, as we can see the reason of the duties required in any of the commandments. I intend to prove this to you before we finish our conversations. But I must not turn aside farther to do it to-night.

Charles. What is the difference between the ceremonial and moral laws?

Mrs. M. One difference is, that the ceremonial laws were designed only for the Jews, while the moral laws are equally binding on every body. The moral laws were engraven on tables of stone by God himself, while the ceremonial laws were taken down from God's mouth, and recorded by Moses.

Charles. Among which of these laws was the fourth commandment placed?

Mrs. M. God engraved it himself on one of the tables of stone among the moral laws, or what are called the ten commandments.

Charles. If men had engraven what was on the

two tables of stone, they might have made a mistake, and put the fourth commandment in the wrong place Or, if it had been printed in a book, and bound up with other laws, the printer or the bookbinder might have made a mistake too. But I do not think God could make a mistake.

Mrs. M. No, my child, it is impossible for God to mistake.

George. And you know too, mother, that when Moses had broken the two tables of stone, on which God had engraven the ten commandments, God gave Moses two more tables, and the fourth commandment was engraven on one of those tables, just as it had been on one of the others. And then, these two tables of stone were laid up in the ark, while the other laws which were written by Moses were only placed in the sanctuary.

Charles. Were there any other laws engraven on the two tables except the fourth commandment, which any body supposes ought to have been placed among the ceremonial laws?

Mrs. M. None, my child. All that believe the Bible, think the rest of the laws are put in the right place, and ought to be kept by every body, as well as by the Jews.

Charles. I believe the fourth commandment was placed where it ought to be, mother.

Mrs. M. If I were to make some rules for you to keep, only while you were recovering from a fit of sickness, and without telling you, should place one of them among other rules which I made for you to keep as long as you live, would you not think it very strange?

George. It would be very strange, mother, but then it would be possible for you to put it there by mistake.

Mrs. M. Yes, my son, I might do so. But suppose I had placed it there on purpose, would you not think that I was not so careful as I ought to be to keep you from error?

George. I should not know what to think, mother.

Mrs. M. If I were very sick, and thought I should soon die, I should call you around my bed, to bid you farewell, and to give you my last counsels. There would be a great many things which I should wish to say to you; I could not tell you a thousandth part of them. I should have strength to mention only a few. Now, if when I was so feeble that I could only just speak, I should say, there are *ten* things which I wish you to do, and should ask one of you to take a pen, and sit by my bed, and write these ten things down, would you not think I wished to have you do them more than any thing else?

Susan. I should, mother, and I should never forget them.

George. All of us would think so, mother.

Mrs. M. Now, my children, God once came down

from heaven, on purpose to tell the Israelites *ten* things which he wished to have them do. He had informed Moses that on the third day he would descend in the sight of all the people, upon Mount Sinai. The Israelites were three days in preparing to meet God. On the third morning there were thunderings and lightnings, and a thick cloud upon the mount, and the voice of the trumpet, exceeding loud, so that all the people in the camp trembled. The smoke of Mount Sinai ascended like the smoke of a furnace, and the whole mountain shook as if rocked by an earthquake. And so terrible was the sight, that even Moses said, I exceedingly fear and quake. The Lord appeared upon the top of Sinai, and in the midst of the clouds, and thunders, and lightnings, spake to the whole host of Israel, who were around the foot of the mount. The words which God spake are recorded in the twentieth chapter of Exodus. They are the ten commandments. The people heard the fourth commandment as distinctly as they heard any of the rest.

When God had given the ten commandments, he ceased to speak. He called Moses up into the mount, and then gave to him the laws which were designed *only for the Jews*, which are called *ceremonial laws*.

Now, can we suppose that the Sabbath, which was given the fourth in order of these ten things, which God came down on Mount Sinai himself to tell the Israelites, was meant only for the Jews, when all the rest were meant for the whole world? By what authority shall we separate what God hath joined together?

There never was a more solemn and terrific scene than that in which God gave the fourth commandment. Fire, darkness, lightnings, thunderings, a loud and terrible voice of a trumpet, all show how God regards the Sabbath, and how dangerous it must be to reject or to break the fourth commandment. It would be no more a violation of God's holy law, to bow down and worship a Hindoo idol—or to take your Maker's name in vain—or to disobey and abuse your parents—or to kill one of your playmates—or to steal—or to lie—than it is to profane the Sabbath. The other commandments were given by the same authority as the fourth—were spoken amidst the same darkness, and lightnings, and thunders—and were engraven by God on the same tables.

Remember this, my dear children, whenever you are tempted to break the Sabbath. If your companions urge you to play with them, or to do any other wrong thing on the Sabbath, think how God spake from the top of Sinai and said—"Remember the Sabbath-day to keep it holy."

The Sabbath is a memorial, or sign, that God made the world. And if God made the world, then, doubtless, he watches over it, and rules it. He made us, and rules us, and watches over us. We are bound to serve and worship him. We are under obligations to please him, and to obey his commandments. He must be glorious and powerful, wise and good. Every Sabbath was fitted to remind men of these truths, and to impress them on their hearts. Can we believe, then, that this memorial was meant only for the Jews?

The fourth commandment occupies a peculiar *place* among the commandments. The first three tell us of our duties to God, and the last six, of our duties to our fellow-men. The Sabbath stands between these two sets of commandments, and binds them together. Without it, neither piety to God, nor love to men, would long exist. An old writer remarks, " The fourth commandment is put into the *bosom* of the decalogue, that it might not be lost —it is the *golden clasp* which joins the two tables together."

I will mention only one more reason, this evening, why I think the Sabbath was not a part of the Jewish ceremonial law, but was designed for all mankind. The Holy Spirit writes the moral law on the hearts and consciences of God's people. This is what God promised. " I will put my laws in their minds, and write them in their hearts." They love God's law. But it is a fact, that good men love the fourth commandment as well as either of the ten. The Sabbath is a precious day to their souls. The more they become like the Saviour, the more they love the Sabbath. The fourth commandment is engraven on the fleshly table of their hearts, as plainly as it was engraven by the finger of God, on the tables of stone. Now, it would be very strange that the Holy Spirit should always engrave the fourth commandment on the hearts of christians as deeply as either of the other commandments, if it ceased to be a law, and became a dead letter, eighteen hundred years ago.

Mrs. M. Before we close our conversation, this evening, let me see, George, whether you remember what reasons I have given, for thinking that God designed the Sabbath to be observed to the end of the world, and by men of all nations.

George. You told us, mother, that if the Sabbath was sanctified at the close of the work of creation, it must be meant for the whole world as much as for the Jews. You said that if it had been meant only for the Jews, it would not have been engraven on the two tables of stone with the other nine commandments which every body ought to keep; and that God would not have spoken it with the other nine commandments on Mount Sinai.

You said that the fourth commandment is placed between the three commandments which teach our duties to God, and the six which teach our duties to men, as if to bind them together; and that without the fourth commandment the other nine would all probably be neglected. You said, too, that when the Holy Spirit writes God's law on the hearts of christians, he writes the fourth commandment as plainly as either of the ten; and that this is strange if the fourth commandment ceased to be binding on men eighteen hundred years ago.

EVENING IV.

SABBATH BINDING ON ALL.

Mother, said Charles, as soon as they were seated, as usual, around the table the next Sabbath evening, Thomas Bradish wanted me to go out into the woods with him to-day, after we got through Sabbath school, and pick up some chesnuts.

Mrs. M. What did you tell him?

Charles. I told him that it was wicked, mother.

Mrs. M. And what did Thomas Bradish say to that?

Charles. He said that nobody would know it, if it was wicked. But I told him God would see us, and be very angry with us, and I would not go with him.

Mrs. M. And what did Thomas say then?

Charles. He said that I was frightened by what my mother told me about the Sabbath. He said his mother never talked to him about keeping the Sabbath, and if she did he would not be so foolish as to mind her.

Mrs. M. Thomas Bradish is a very wicked boy to talk so, and I fear he will come to no good end. But did Thomas go into the woods after chesnuts?

Charles. Yes, mother, I saw him and another boy, going across the fields, toward the mountain, just as the bell began to ring for meeting.

Mrs. M. Do you think, Charles, that Thomas Bradish and the other boy would have dared to go to Mount Sinai, and climb up into the trees after chesnuts, if there had been any there, when the dark clouds were all around the top of the mountain, and the lightnings were flashing thick, and the thunder roaring very loud, and God was commanding the people to remember the Sabbath-day to keep it holy?

Charles. No, mother, he would have been terrified, as the Israelites were, and wanted to fly as far from the mountain as he could.

Mrs. M. But, Charles, God was as near, when Thomas Bradish went to get chesnuts on the mountain, to-day, as he was to the people of Israel when he came down on Mount Sinai, and gave the fourth commandment. And though it did not thunder and lighten, and though Thomas Bradish did not hear any voice from the top of the mountain, telling him to remember the Sabbath-day to keep it holy, God was just as angry as he would have been if Thomas Bradish had gone to Mount Sinai to look for fruit, on the next Sabbath after God gave the ten commandments to Israel.

Here Mrs. M. was called to the door;—when she returned she said,

You ought to be very thankful, Charles, that you did not go with Thomas Bradish and break the Sabbath to-day. He fell down from a tree this afternoon, and was almost killed.

Charles. Did he, mother?

Mrs. M. I have just heard so. One of his neighbors has come, in haste, to get your father to go and dress his wounds. The man said, that Thomas and the other boy wandered over the mountain till almost night, without finding many chesnuts. There had not been frost enough to open the burs. At last they came to a high tree which was loaded with chesnuts. They tried to beat them off with clubs and long poles, but they could not get many in that way. So Thomas said he would climb up into the tree, and shake some off. The other boy told him he had better not, for the branches were slender and would easily break. But Thomas said he would not come so far, and look so long, and go home without any chesnuts in his pockets. So he climbed up into the tree and began to shake. He went out too far on one of the limbs, and it broke. Thomas caught hold of another limb, but that broke too, and he fell to the ground. He was hurt badly, and if he escapes with his life, he must be very thankful.

Susan. I am glad that our mother tells us to keep the Sabbath, are not you, Charles?

Mrs. M. Children are very apt to think their parents make them keep the Sabbath too strictly. But Thomas Bradish will wish, to-night, that his mother had taught him to observe the Sabbath better. Poor boy! I hope he will learn from this accident to "remember the Sabbath day to keep it holy;" and I hope, too, that his mother will learn to be more faithful in giving good advice to her children.

Charles. Are there not more people wounded and killed on the Sabbath than on any other day?

Mrs. M. A great many accidents happen on the Sabbath. I see some mentioned in the newspapers almost every week. I think there are more, in proportion to the number of people employed in labor, and in amusements, and on excursions of pleasure, than on other days.

There is something striking in the many accidents that happen on the Sabbath. It would be dreadful to be taken out of the world while violating one of the commandments of God.

George. But, mother, uncle John says, that the accidents which happen on the Sabbath would happen, in the same circumstances, on any other day. He says accidents are no proof that God is angry with those who break the fourth commandment, or that it is still binding.

Mrs. M. I know, my son, that this is not a world in which God rewards men, fully, according to what they do; and that we ought to be cautious how we think God is more angry with men who meet with accidents and misfortunes, than he is with others. But the Bible tells us that God in former days sometimes cut down men suddenly when they were guilty of great sins. When God did so, he was said to punish men by special judgments. When we see similar things happening now, we cannot tell that he does not punish men in the same way. The best people in the world have thought that God sometimes punishes, now, by special judgments, those who are very bold and daring in sin. When, for example, a profane person dies, instantly, with an oath on his tongue, they think that if the reason of his sudden death was given, as the reason for the death of some wicked men is given in the Bible, it would appear that God cut him down, by a special judgment, for his profaneness.

Your uncle John says that the same accidents would happen, in similar circumstances, on any other day as well as on the Sabbath. I have no doubt that they sometimes would. For instance, a party of thoughtless young men and women take a sail-boat and go out into some bay, or on to some lake, for pleasure, on the Sabbath. They do not know how to manage the boat. They are not used to trimming the sails and turning the rudder about. They cannot guide the boat as old sailors would. A light gale springs up, and they know not what to do. They get frightened, perhaps, and through their mismanagement, the boat upsets and they are drowned.

I suppose the same things would happen sometimes on any other day of the week, as well as on the Sabbath. But does this show that they were not drowned as a punishment for their Sabbath-breaking? If you eat too much, you will suffer for it. The glutton may have the gout, or some other disease, in consequence of high living. But this is a punishment. God works no miracle in punishing the glutton. The gout comes in the natural course of things; but it is none the less a punishment, and none the easier to bear, for that.

So we might say of the sailing party, even if they were not drowned by a special judgment. Would the drowning, on the Sabbath, be any easier, for coming in the natural order of things? Would it be any the less a punishment?

If the glutton had let high living alone, he would,

not have had the gout; and if the sailing party had kept the Sabbath as they ought, they would not have been drowned.

And do not think, my children, because you may break the Sabbath once or twice, or several times, and not be punished, that God will never punish you. You will certainly be punished at last, and may be punished yet in this world. I suppose that all the sailing party had often been guilty of breaking the Sabbath, before the day on which they were drowned. But they did not hear any thunder, or see any lightning, to show that God was angry with them for profaning his holy day, and they thought he never would punish them. So they grew bolder and bolder, and more and more hardened, until they thought they would make a sailing party on the Sabbath. They did so, and were drowned. But if they had minded what their parents or Sabbath-school teachers told them, when they broke the Sabbath at first, by going with wicked boys and girls to play, they would not have gone on this party. So you see they were punished at last for what they did long before.

But I have a few things more to say to you about the fourth commandment. There are two more objections, George, that your uncle John makes, which I promised you, last week, I would answer to-night, as I was too busy to answer them then. You may mention them.

George. Uncle John said that the Sabbath was not known before the time of Moses; for the Bible declares that God gave it to the children of Israel as *a sign of the covenant he had made with them.*

Mrs. M. The Bible does say so several times, but I think this does not show that the Sabbath had never been known before the Israelites came out of Egypt, or that it was not meant for others besides the Jews. Do you think, George, that there never was any rain on the earth for sixteen hundred and fifty years before the flood?

George. I have no doubt there was; for if there had been no rain there would have been no water to drink, and the fields would have been parched and dried up.

Charles. But you told us, mother, one evening, that there is not rain very often in some parts of Egypt. But Egypt is a very fertile country.

Mrs. M. Do not the fields in Egypt need any water?

Charles. O yes, mother, the fields need water, but they get water for them out of the Nile.

Mrs. M. And where does the Nile get water?

Charles. I do not know—I have not thought of that.

Mrs. M. The water of the Nile comes from heavy rains among the mountains in Abyssinia, where the Nile, which is a very long river, rises. But I think if there should be no rain for a few years in Abyssinia, there would not be much water in the Nile, for the fields, or for the cattle, or for man.

Charles. There must have been rain then, mother, before the flood; but I wonder what rain before the flood has to do with the fourth commandment.

Mrs. M. You must not be too impatient, Charles, if you wish to learn. I shall show you very soon why I asked George whether there was any rain before the flood.

Can you tell me, George, what makes the rainbow?

George. The rays of the sun refracted from the drops of rain in a cloud.

Mrs. M. Then there must have been rainbows before the flood.

George. Yes, mother, a great many times.

Susan. How beautiful Adam and Eve must have thought the rainbow, when they first saw it painted on the dark cloud!

Mrs. M. When Noah had come out of the ark, God said to him, "I will establish my covenant with you; and this is the *token* of the covenant which I make between me and you—I do set my bow in the clouds, and it shall be for a token of a covenant between me and the earth." Now, by a token here, God means the same thing that he means by a sign, of his covenant with Israel.

Charles. O mother, now I begin to see why

you asked George about the rain before the flood

Mrs. M. As the rainbow, which was almost as old as the world, was set in the cloud for a sign of God's covenant with Noah, so the Sabbath, which had been two thousand five hundred years in existence, was given as a sign of God's covenant with the Israelites.

Now, George, you may mention the other objection made by your uncle John.

George. He said that the fourth commandment has expired of itself, or else has been repealed; for Paul told the Colossians that the Sabbath-days are "a shadow of things to come," and reproved the Galatians because they observed days, and months, and times, and years.

Mrs. M. If a law is limited to some particular time, when that time arrives it is a law no longer, and is said to expire by its own limitation. For example, if Congress, for some reason, should think fit to make a law that no vessel should sail from any port in the United States for sixty days; when the sixty days ended, the law would cease to be binding. It might be said to die or to expire, and vessels might sail without leave from Congress. There would be no law against it. It would be as lawful for them to sail, as though a law forbidding them to sail for sixty days had never been made.

But Congress might make a law that vessels should not sail from any port in the United States, without saying how long the law should last. If such a law was made, it would be binding until Congress should repeal it, or say it was a law no longer.

Now it is not said, in the fourth commandment, how long it should be binding. It is not said that it should be a law for a thousand years, or two thousand years, or until the Messiah came.

It would, therefore, never cease to be a law until repealed by the same authority that made it. It would never expire by its own limitation.

Well, then, has God repealed the fourth commandment?—Has he said it shall not be a law any longer? Your uncle John and others who think as he does, quote several passages from Paul's Epistles, to show that the fourth commandment has been repealed. I need not examine every one of them, for what I shall say on one of the passages, will apply to the others.

I will take what Paul says in Colossians, 2 : 16, 17—" Let no man, therefore, judge you in meat, or in drink, or in respect of a holy day, or of the new moon, or of the Sabbath days, which are a shadow of things to come : but the body is Christ."

George. I did not know, mother, that Paul wrote so about the Sabbath.

Mrs. M. The Jewish feasts are often called Sabbaths in the Old Testament, and some suppose Paul, in this passage, meant these feasts, and not the weekly Sabbath. But I do not think this very probable.

The Jews who early became Christians, were very fond of their old customs and modes of worship. They were particularly fond of the Sabbath. The Gentiles who became Christians, kept the *first day* of the week, as the day of rest. This, at that time, was called the "*Lord's day*," to distinguish it from the *Jewish Sabbath*. The Jews, too, kept the Lord's day: but some of them, also, kept the seventh day, which was their former Sabbath. Those Jews who kept both days, wanted that the Gentiles should do the same. When they lived in the same neighborhood, and belonged to the same church with Gentiles, I have no doubt they sometimes talked about them harshly, for not resting on both days. Paul did not believe the Gentiles were under obligation to keep the seventh day, or Jewish Sabbath. He was willing that the Gentiles should observe it, as well as the Christian Sabbath, or Lord's day, if they chose to keep both. But he would not let the Jews compel them to keep the seventh day. He would have every man do as he pleased in regard to keeping it. This was the reason why he said to the Colossians, " Let no man judge you in meat, or in drink, or in respect of a holy day, or of the new moon, or of the Sabbath days."

Paul knew that the Jewish temple and nation would soon be destroyed, and that then the Jewish ceremonies and institutions would speedily be forgotten. For the sake of peace, therefore, he let the Jews keep the seventh day, their former Sabbath; but then they must also keep the Lord's day.

It was not the day of rest which Paul says was "a shadow of things to come." It was only the *Jewish Sabbath*. The christian Sabbath, which was already kept on the first day of the week, was not repealed; but it remains, and will remain, as in the time of Paul, till days and weeks are known no more.

This is a very interesting part of our subject, my children, and as we can spend a little time longer in conversation this evening, I will mention one or two more reasons why I think Paul did not mean to repeal the Sabbath.

The apostles contended against the ceremonial law of the Jews, and said that it was never designed for the Gentiles. They preached against it, and wrote against it, as much as was necessary and proper in their circumstances. They said that Christ had blotted it out, that it was *waxing old*, and *ready to vanish away*.

Now, my dear children, look at what has happened, and see if it corresponds with what the apostles said should come to pass. The rites of the ceremonial law, the many washings, the division of meats into clean and unclean, all vanished away long since from the christian church—Christ has blotted them out. This is just what Paul said would happen. *But has the Sabbath vanished away?* Far from it. Paul kept it himself, and taught others to keep it by his example. The other apostles kept it, and the earliest saints and martyrs kept it. It has been kept from that day to this, and the fourth commandment seems no more likely to vanish away from the church of Christ than any other commandment of the ten. I should not know why this is so, if I believed, with your uncle John, that the fourth commandment was repealed as long ago as the days of Paul. I think it is very evident that the Sabbath, which has fared so differently from the ceremonial law, was no part of this law. I think that the Sabbath, which has so long outlived what the apostle calls the hand-writing of ordinances, is no part of these ordinances. I am, therefore, fully satisfied that your uncle John gives a wrong meaning to the words of Paul.

George. The prophets foretold many things which would happen in the church of Christ. Do they ever foretell, mother, that there would be any Sabbath kept then?

Mrs. M. Yes, my son, Isaiah, in the fifty-sixth chapter of his prophecy, says, there would be a Sabbath among the Gentiles, who would be converted to God. The chapter is a short and beautiful one, and I hope all of you will read it to-night, before you retire to rest. Certain persons were prohibited, by the ceremonial law, from coming into the congregation of the Lord. Of these, God says that if they will keep his Sabbaths, "even unto them will I give in my house, and within my walls, a place and a name better than of sons and of daughters." This shows that the Sabbath would outlive the ceremonial law, and be blessed by God in the christian church.

And why should not the Sabbath exist in the Christian as well as in the Jewish church? I have told you already that men need it in every age and in every country. And would God take away from his church so great a blessing, which it had long enjoyed?

And the Sabbath is not only as much needed in the Christian church as it was in the Jewish, but it can be made even more useful now than it was at that time. The Jews did not have so many means of making the Sabbath profitable as God has given to the Christian church. God has revealed his will more clearly to us than he revealed it to them. They lived in the twilight. We live in the full light of noonday. The Holy Spirit is now shed forth more abundantly on men than before the death of our Saviour, and greater numbers are converted to God by the preaching of the Gospel. But men must assemble together, or there can be no public preaching, and they would not assemble if there was no Sabbath. To the Jew, the Sabbath was the brightest among many stars; to the Christian, it is the sun in the firmament, shining in all its glory.

You might almost as well close every church, and destroy every Bible, and seal the lips of every minister in christian lands, as to abolish the Sabbath, or have it regarded only as made by man. It is now the special day for prayer, for communion with God, for self-examination, for religious reading and meditation; and more persons, probably, become pious, from the divine blessing on the public and private services of the Sabbath, than on the means employed during all the other days of the week. If God, then, did not mean to have the Sabbath binding on all, but only on the Jews, it would almost appear to show a want of wisdom or of goodness. Man would, in such a case, seem to be, in this matter, wiser or more benevolent than God; for man would then, of his own accord, have continued a valuable and necessary institution, from which God had withdrawn the sanction of his authority.

God must, too, I think, have meant that the Sabbath should be binding on all, to the end of time, as well as on the Jews, or else he would not so constantly distinguish it with his favor. Why does he let his people love the Sabbath so well? and why does he continue to bless so richly the services of that day, if he designed the Sabbath only for the Jews, and recalled his command to keep it nearly two thousand years ago? I cannot believe that he has recalled his command, and so I must think that when he spake from Sinai, and said, "Remember the Sabbath-day to keep it holy," he meant to bind you, and me, and every person, in every age, to keep the Sabbath, just as much as he bound those who heard the trumpet, and saw the clouds and lightnings around the top of the mount, when the fourth commandment was originally given.

I have dwelt the longer on this part of our subject, because I wished to convince you that the Sabbath is not now, as some assert, merely a day which it is *expedient* to keep, but that it is a day which God has *commanded* to be kept till the end of time. If men think that God has not required them, in this age, to observe the Sabbath, they will be likely, often, to neglect or violate it; nothing will restrain them from this but the warning voice of God, "Remember the Sabbath day, to keep it holy."

And to the christian it is not a matter of indifference, whether God still regards the Sabbath with peculiar favor. The christian loves to think, when the Sabbath comes, that he can look for the special blessing of God on his worship, his meditations, and his reading; for God, who cannot lie, has promised such a blessing. Prove to the christian that no such promise has been made, and you would fill his bosom with sadness. He would still love the Sabbath—he would still delight in its duties, but he could not say with a gushing heart, "*This is the day which the Lord hath made*, we will rejoice and be glad in it."

EVENING V.

CHANGE OF THE SABBATH.

George. You told us, mother, in our former conversations, that the fourth commandment was meant for all other nations, as well as for the Jews.

Mrs. M. Yes, my son.

George. And you told us that it had never been repealed, and so must be binding now.

Mrs. M. Yes, I told you that, too.

George. Well, then, mother, why do not good people keep the fourth commandment?

Mrs. M. Do not good people keep it, my son?

George. No, mother, I do not see that they do. The fourth commandment says, "The seventh day is the Sabbath of the Lord thy God." But we keep the first day of the week as the Sabbath, and we work on the seventh day, in which God says, "Thou shalt not do any work." Is not this to break the fourth commandment?

Mrs. M. This is what we will converse about this evening. I will try to show you why we keep the first day of the week as the Sabbath, and not the seventh day, and that this is no breach of the fourth commandment.

Time has been divided into three periods. The first of these three periods is called the *Patriarchal*, and extends from the creation to Moses. The second is called the *Mosaical*, or *Jewish*, and extends from Moses to Christ. The third is called the *Christian*, and extends from the time of our Saviour to the end of the world.

During the first and second of these periods the Sabbath was a sign or memorial to make men keep in mind *some great event*. During the first or *Patriarchal* period, it was a sign of God's resting on the seventh day, after he had created the world. The Sabbath began on the day in which God rested, and came every seventh day.

During the second, the *Mosaical* or *Jewish* period, beside being a sign of God's resting from the work of creation, it was *also a sign of the release of the Jews from their bondage in Egypt.* God says to the Jews (Deuteronomy, 5 : 15,) "And remember that thou wast a servant in the land of Egypt, and that the Lord thy God brought thee out thence, through a mighty hand and by a stretched out arm; *therefore*, the Lord thy God commanded thee to keep the Sabbath day." Learned men say it is highly probable that the exact reckoning of time, from the creation, was lost by the Israelites during their heavy bondage, and that they *began to reckon their Sabbaths from the day when they came out of Egypt.*

During the third, or the *Christian* period, it is natural, therefore, to expect the Sabbath would be a memorial of some great event, and would, as in the two former cases, be reckoned from the day in which that event happened. Such an event is the resurrection of the Lord Jesus Christ from the dead. If the creation of the world was worthy to be kept in mind by a memorial like the Sabbath, the redemption of the world by Jesus Christ is equally worthy. Indeed, the Bible represents it as more worthy. "Behold I create new heavens, and a new earth; and the former heavens shall not be remembered nor come to mind." The prophet, in this passage, seems to mean, that the work of redeeming the world from sin is more glorious than the first creation, and should be commemorated in its stead by the same sign. This sign is the Sabbath. From what the prophet says, then, as well as from what was done during the two former periods, we are led, I think, to expect a change in the day of keeping the Sabbath.

George. Has the day, then, been changed?

Mrs. M. I think there is evidence enough that it has.

Our Saviour appeared to his disciples, soon after he arose from the dead, on the first day of the week. The first day of the next week he appeared to them again, as they were assembled, and probably for worship.

The day of Pentecost was on the first day of the week, when the promise of Christ to send the Holy Spirit to his disciples was fulfilled. The first day of the week was kept as the Sabbath in the time of the apostles. Paul, at Troas, met with the church when they came together, on the first day of the week, to break bread. He tells the Corinthians to lay by them in store, for the poor saints, on the first day of the week, as God had prospered them. He gave the same order to the churches in Galatia. The apostle John speaks of one day of the week as familiarly known, when he wrote, by the name of the Lord's day. "I was," says he, "in the Spirit on the Lord's day." That this was the first day of the week, I have no doubt; and that it was so called on account of the resurrection of Christ from the dead on that day.

George. But, mother, you have not mentioned any command of the Lord Jesus Christ, or of his apostles, to change the seventh day for the first. Why was there not a direct command to make the change, if God meant it should be made?

Mrs. M. It is true that I have not mentioned any direct command for this change,—nor is there any in the Bible. But, my son, the apostles were inspired by God to instruct his people in their duty,—and do you suppose they would change the day of keeping the Sabbath, or suffer the churches to change the day, if God had not shown them that it was his will to have the change take place?

George. No, mother, I think they would never have done that.

Mrs. M. The example of the apostles, in such a case, is as binding on us as a command would be,—for it shows clearly what the will of God is.

George. But, mother, it would have been so easy to record a command in the Bible, that I wonder it was omitted. Then there would be no disputes in the world about what day men ought to keep as the Sabbath.

Mrs. M. Men will never be in want of something to dispute about, so long as they dislike the truth. God knows best how much ought to be recorded in the Bible, and though many persons wonder why God did not have more said in the Bible, on some points, I have no doubt that the Bible is better as it is now, than men could make it

George. But, mother, do you know of any reason why there was no direct command given by the apostles for changing the Sabbath from the seventh to the first day of the week?

Mrs. M. One reason was, the peculiar state of the church at that time. The Jews were very fond, as I have told you already, of their customs, and of none more than of the Sabbath. If the change from the seventh to the first day had been made suddenly, and by express command, the Jews would have been much offended. They would have had strong prejudices against the Gospel; and might for this very reason have rejected it. The apostles knew that in a little time all these Jewish customs would be swept away; and as there was nothing positively wrong in keeping the seventh day, they suffered the Jews to keep that, together with the first. Just so they suffered the Jews to keep the passover, as well as to celebrate the Lord's Supper. But when the temple was left without one stone upon another, the Jewish priesthood, and altars, and sacrifices, and Sabbaths, all disappeared. The Lord's day took the place of the Jewish Sabbath; and the first day took the place of the seventh, as a day of rest.

George. Do early writers give any account of this change? I should think that if there was such a change as you have told us of to-night, they would mention it.

Mrs. M. They do mention it, my son. Ignatius, about the year of our Lord 101, calls the first day of the week " the Lord's day, the day consecrated to the resurrection, the queen and prince of all days!" He says, too, "Let every friend of Christ celebrate the *Lord's day*." Pliny the younger, in a letter to the emperor Trajan, in the year of our Lord 107, says that the christians were accustomed, "on a *stated* day, to meet before daylight, and to repeat among themselves a hymn to Christ as to a God." The Roman persecutors were accustomed to put this question to the martyrs, "Have you kept the Lord's day?" showing that the early christians did so. In the year of our Lord 147, Justin Martyr, in an apology addressed to the emperor Antoninus, in which he would be careful to state nothing but what was true, says, "On the day called *Sunday*, there is a meeting in one place, of all the christians who live either in towns or in the country. Every one of us christians keeps the Sabbath, meditating in the law and rejoicing in the works of God." Eusebius, the great writer of Church History in ancient times, says, about the year of our Lord 320—"On each day of our Saviour's resurrection, that is, on every first day of the week, which is called *Lord's day*, we may see those who partake of the consecrated food, and that body (of Christ) bowing down to him." He says, also, that "*all things whatsoever it was duty to do on the Sabbath*," that is, the Jewish seventh day, "THESE WE HAVE TRANSFERRED TO THE LORD'S DAY AS MORE APPROPRIATELY BELONGING TO IT."

He says, also, that it was handed down to them

from former times, that they should meet on the Lord's day. Many other ancient writers say the same. It is as evident as any thing can make it, that the apostles and early christians kept the first day of the week as the Sabbath. And they never would have done this, if they had not good authority. We keep the first day because they kept it, and because we believe they would never have changed the day, without knowing such was the will of God.

I will mention only one more reason for thinking that the Sabbath has been changed from the seventh to the first day of the week, by divine authority. It is this: God bestows the same blessing on the first day, now, which he originally promised to the seventh; and I cannot believe he would do this, if men had altered the day of keeping the Sabbath without his permission. By distinguishing the first day of the week so highly with his favor, he shows, I think, that he approves the change.

I will now try to show you that this change is not a breach of the fourth commandment.

You told us, George, in our first conversation, that God was six days in making the world, because he meant to have men work six days before they had a day of rest; and Charles told us, that the reason given in the fourth commandment why God sanctified the Sabbath, is, that he rested on the seventh day after he had finished making the world.

The Sabbath, therefore, was a memorial of the work of creation. But, George, if it had been kept on any other day beside that which the Jews called the seventh, might it not have been a memorial of the creation just as well?

George. I think so, mother.

Mrs. M. And would it not teach men just as well that they ought to rest, if kept on any other day, as if kept on the seventh?

George. I think so, mother.

Mrs. M. Then if the commandment had been, " Thou shalt work six days, and then rest one day; and then thou shalt work six days more, and rest another day," and so on, you think the Sabbath might have been just as well kept, after the fourth commandment was given, on the day which the Jews called the sixth, or the fifth, as on the seventh?

George. I do not see why it might not, mother.

Mrs. M. Well, then, let us look at the fourth commandment, and see whether it is not so expressed, that the day may be changed without breaking the commandment, or changing its design. You may repeat the first part of it, George.

George. " Remember the Sabbath day to keep it holy."

Mrs. M. So we can remember the *Sabbath day*, to keep it holy, just as well on any *other* day as the *seventh* without breaking the fourth commandment, *if we have evidence that we ought to keep the Sabbath on some other day.* You may repeat the next part of the commandment, Charles.

Charles. "Six days shalt thou labor and do all thy work."

Mrs. M. This part of the commandment would be kept just as well if we were to observe the Sabbath on the first day of the week as on the seventh day. It is not said *which* of the seven days we shall devote to labor, but only that we shall work six days, and rest one. So this part of the commandment does not hinder a change in the day for keeping the Sabbath. What is in the next part of the commandment, Susan?

Susan. "But the seventh day is the Sabbath of the Lord thy God."

Mrs. M. This, you will observe, only says that the seventh day was, AT THAT TIME, the day of rest—it does not say it always should be the day of rest. The seventh day answers the purposes of the Sabbath no better than either of the other days would. If God pleased, he might change the day of keeping the Sabbath, without repealing the command to keep *one day in seven* as holy. For you must remember that the Sabbath, as a season of holy rest, is one thing; and the day on which it is kept, another. Besides, as an able writer remarks, "The christian Sabbath, in the sense of the fourth commandment, is as much the seventh day, as the

Jewish Sabbath was the seventh day. It is kept after six days' labor, as that was. It is the seventh day, reckoning from the beginning of our first working day, as well as their Sabbath was the seventh day, reckoning from the beginning of their first working day."

Suppose a part of the Jewish nation, after receiving the fourth commandment, had removed to the Sandwich Islands. If you will look on the map, you will see that these islands lie nearly on the opposite side of the earth from Palestine, where the Jews lived. I suppose it is noon at the Sandwich Islands about the same time that it is midnight in Palestine. And when it is sunset in Palestine, I suppose it is about sunrise at the Sandwich Islands. The Jews began their day at evening. Soon after the sun had set, the Jews in Palestine would regard the Sabbath as begun—for the seventh day had come. But when should the Jews in the Sandwich Islands begin their Sabbath? Should they begin it when the evening begins in the Sandwich Islands, or when the evening begins in Palestine? I think they would, without doubt, begin the Sabbath when evening begins in the Sandwich Islands. But then they would keep only half of the same seventh day which their brethren keep in Palestine. The other half would be a part of what is the first day in Palestine.

The Jews, at the present time, keep the seventh

day as the Sabbath. Suppose that a Jew should sail from London, around Cape Horn, and across the Pacific and Indian Oceans, and around the Cape of Good Hope, and then back to London. He would lose one day, and his Saturday, or seventh day, would be Sunday, or the first day of the week in London. He would keep his seventh day as the Sabbath all the while he was on the voyage. He might keep it still when he got home. The christians of London would keep the first day of the week as the Sabbath while he was gone, and they would continue to keep it after his return. And yet after his return, the Jew and the christians of London would keep the very same time as the Sabbath; though one would call it Saturday and the others would call it Sunday, and one would call it the seventh day, while the others would call it the first day.

George. If those who wish to keep the seventh day as the Sabbath in this country, would only sail westward around the world, when they got back they would keep the same time as the Sabbath which we keep; and then they would not disturb our Sabbaths, and we should not disturb them.

Mrs. M. Yes, my son, and if we, too, were to sail around the world the other way, when we got back our first day would be their seventh day, and then we should not disturb each other.

I think now you will regard the exact day on

which the Sabbath is kept, as in itself unimportant, except so far as the will of God is known.

George. Why, then, did God command the Jews to keep the seventh day? Why not let them keep any other day in the week which they chose?

Mrs. M. God must command men to keep the same day, for if he did not, one might keep the Sabbath on Monday, and another on Tuesday, and another on Wednesday, and so on through all the days of the week. They would be continually disturbing each other, and a great part of the benefits of the Sabbath would be lost.

The change of the day, from the seventh to the first is not, then, in any proper sense, a repeal of the fourth commandment. Nor is it a breach of it to work on the seventh day; because we have good evidence that since the resurrection of our Saviour the time for keeping the Sabbath has been changed by divine appointment, that is, by the order of God, from the seventh to the first day of the week.

EVENING VI.

SABBATH NECESSARY FOR THE BODY.

Susan. How beautifully the fire burns in the grate this evening, mother.

Mrs. M. Yes, my dear, this is a beautiful world we live in, and how well fitted one thing is to another.

Susan. What do you mean, mother?

Mrs. M. If that coal in the grate were as hard as stone, it would not give out heat enough to do us any good. And then, again, if it gave out a hundred times more heat, I suppose it would melt the grate. It is as well fitted as it can be to the grate, and to our wants.

Susan. But God did not make the grate, did he, mother?

Mrs. M. No, a man made the grate, but God made the iron of which it is formed.

How well fitted the ground is to our use! If it was as soft as a marsh, we could not walk about upon it. And if it was hard as a rock, we could not plough it, and get grain and vegetables to eat.

And how well fitted the cattle are to our wants. If they were no larger than sheep, they would not have strength enough to draw carts and logs. And if they were fifty or sixty feet long, as some animals were, whose bones are now and then found, they would be so large that we could not manage them. If the cows were ten or fifteen feet high, how inconvenient it would be to milk them; and if the handsome colt which your father gave George the other day should grow to be as tall as one of the cherry-trees in our fruit garden, how could George ever contrive to mount upon his back?

And the light, too, how well fitted it is for the eye! It goes two hundred thousand miles in a second. Light is matter, as much as a table is matter—only it is made up of very, very little particles. But if the particles of light were as large as the point of a needle, moving so swiftly, they would batter out our eyes every time we open our eyelids. I could not look a minute at my dear Susan without losing my sight. How well fitted one thing is to another in this beautiful world which God has made, and how well fitted every thing is to the use of man!

Susan. O how glad I am light is so well fitted to our eyes, that I can look at my dear mother and not be made blind, as my cousin Jane is!

Mrs. M. You ought to be quite as glad that God has made the Sabbath—for it is just as well fitted for man, as the light is to the eye. *And this is what we will converse about this evening. I shall try to show you the fitness of the Sabbath to man's nature and condition.*

George. Do you expect, mother, to show that the Sabbath is fitted for man's use, as the light is to the eye, or the size of oxen and horses to our strength?

Mrs. M. Certainly I do, George. Why should there not be such a fitness? Why should we not expect it? For God, who made the light for our eyes, and oxen for our use, *also made the Sabbath for man!* I think we might expect to find the Sabbath perfectly fitted for man's use, perfectly suited to his wants and condition.

George. I shall be glad to have you show this, mother; for uncle John said, the other day, it was a useless waste of time. He said that if a man lived to be seventy years old, and kept every Sabbath, it would amount to ten years. This, he said, was a great deal of time; and his life was already too short to have so long a piece cut off from it.

Mrs. M. And what did you tell him?

George. I told him I did not believe he would gain any thing by breaking the Sabbath; and that though I could not answer his objection then, I hoped I should be able to answer it before my mother had finished her conversations about the Sabbath.

Mrs. M. Does your uncle John ever sleep any?

George. Sleep, mother! Why, he must sleep every night like other people. And besides that, he sleeps some every day; for the last time I went to see him I found him asleep. He said, while he sat in his easy chair rubbing his eyes, that I was young and vigorous now, but when I was as old as he, I should find a short nap after dinner a very comfortable thing.

Mrs. M. I suppose your uncle John sleeps, then, about eight hours in a day. This is a great deal to take out every day from the time of one whose life is so short! At this rate he would spend one-third of his short life in sleep—what a waste!

George. But, mother, men must sleep, they cannot help it.

Mrs. M. I know it, my son; but this does not show that sleep is any more fitted to the nature of man than the Sabbath is. Nor does it show that it is less a waste of time to sleep, than to keep the Sabbath. It only shows that a man can get along awhile without keeping the Sabbath better than he can without sleeping. But it does not show that in the end he will not suffer from violating the Sabbath, as really as he would from want of sleep. If your uncle John were kept from sleeping three or four nights at a time, he would suffer for it immediately. He would break one of the laws of his nature, for God has made him so that he needs sleep, and he would be punished at once. If he were to keep no Sabbath for three or four years, but work hard every day, he would also break a law of his nature, as he did by not sleeping,—for God has made him so that his body needs the Sabbath. And I think he would suffer for it; he would be punished for it as really as he was punished for not sleeping, only the punishment would be longer in coming. He would grow old faster than if he rested on the Sabbath. He would wear out sooner. This would be one part of his punishment.

George. What makes you think, mother, that God has made men so that their bodies need the rest of the Sabbath as really as their bodies need sleep?

Mrs. M. Because I have the same kind of evidence that men need rest on the Sabbath, as that they need sleep. What evidence have you that men need sleep?

George. Every body sleeps,—and besides, when any one's rest is broken for several nights, he suffers for it. And those who should be often broken of their rest would not live as long as if they slept soundly every night.

Mrs. M. Well, George, I have the same kind of evidence that men need to rest on the Sabbath. When they rest on the Sabbath, they are more vigorous than when they do not rest. They are more healthy. They can do more work, for they are stronger, and they live longer.

George. If this is so, mother, then the Sabbath is indeed fitted for man's use, as much as light is fitted for the eye.

Mrs. M. It is said by writers on slavery, that the

lives of slaves were cut short, especially in the West Indies, by constant labor.

George. But were the slaves made to work on the Sabbath?

Mrs. M. They were not compelled by their masters to work on the Sabbath; but then they labored for their own support, and went to market on the Sabbath, after they had worked hard six days for their masters. The climate was favorable to their health—but this constant labor, it is said, shortened their life.

Mr. Henry R. Schoolcraft gives an account of an expedition which he made, with twenty men, to examine the Upper Mississippi, in the summer of 1830. He went on another tour in the summer of 1832. He says, "No Sabbath-day was employed in travelling. It was laid down as a principle, to rest on that day, and wherever it overtook us, whether on the land or on the water, the men knew that their labor would cease, and that the day would be given them for rest. It may, perhaps, be thought that the giving up of one-seventh part of the whole time employed on a public expedition in a very remote region, and with many men to subsist, must have, in this ratio, increased the time devoted to the route. But the result was far otherwise. The time devoted to recruit the men not only gave the surgeon of the party an opportunity to heal up the bruises and chafings they complained of, but it replenished them with strength; they commenced the weekly labor with renewed zest, and this zest was, in a measure, kept up by the reflection that the ensuing Sabbath would be a day of rest. It was found, by computing the whole route, and comparing the time employed with that which had been devoted on similar routes in this part of the world, that an equal space had been gone over in less time than it had ever been known to be performed by loaded canoes, or (as the fact is) by light canoes, before." I give you the account in his own language; and it is a striking proof that nothing is lost by keeping, and nothing gained by breaking, the Sabbath. For here was a long, fatiguing journey, made in less time, by resting on the Sabbath, than if they had traveled every day.

You remember, George, that we read the other night, that in the revolution in France about forty years ago, the French thought they would not have any Sabbath like ours. So they divided the week into nine days of labor and one day of rest. But it is said that they found men could not do so much work, and were more wearied when they rested only one day in ten, than when they rested one day in seven.

The celebrated Dr. Spurzheim says, "The cessation of labor one day in seven contributes to the preservation of health, and to the restoration of the bodily powers." Your uncle John cannot say that

Dr. Spurzheim wrote so because he was a bigot, and was prejudiced in favor of the Sabbath; for Dr. Spurzheim was not at all strict in his religious notions, or in his views of the Sabbath. He was a very learned and scientific man, and would not have said what he did about the Sabbath unless he thought he had good reasons.

Dr. Rush, of Philadelphia, one of the ablest physicians that have ever been in the United States, and a fine scholar, says, "If there were no hereafter, individuals and societies would be great gainers by attending public worship. Rest from labor, in the house of God, winds up the machine of the soul and body better than any thing else, and thereby invigorates it for the labors and duties of the ensuing week."

George. I will tell uncle John what Dr. Rush says. I hope he will not think any longer that it is a waste of time to keep the Sabbath.

Mrs. M. A year or two ago the British Parliament took up the subject of observing the Sabbath. They appointed a committee to examine the matter. On this committee were some of the most distinguished members of parliament. The parliament wanted to learn whether it does men any good, in this world, to keep the Sabbath.

You see they were not inquiring whether God has commanded men to keep the Sabbath. I suppose some of the members of parliament did not much care whether the fourth commandment is now binding or not. But if the Sabbath does any good to men in this world, when it is well kept, they wanted the British nation should enjoy the benefit. The committee put questions to a great many men of different trades and professions, to get information about the Sabbath. They examined, among others, one of the most eminent physicians in London, called Dr. Farre. He was a skillful man, and the committee asked him many questions. I cannot tell you all he said, though it is very interesting. I will tell you a part of it in my own language. He said the Sabbath does men good in this world, as well as in the next. He said that the rest which men get by sleeping in the night, is not as much as they need to keep them healthy, and give them long life. He said it is very kind, therefore, in God, to give men one day in seven for rest, that they may get recruited. Try an experiment, he said, on beasts that labor. Take the horse, for example. Work him for some time, as much as you can make him bear, every day in the week. Do not let him rest on the Sabbath. Then work him for the same length of time again, and just as hard, only let him lie still on the Sabbath. You will soon see that he is more vigorous, and works better, when he rests on the Sabbath, than when he works seven days in the week.

Charles. Now I see, mother, why God commanded that the *cattle* should not be made to work on the Sabbath.

Susan. Why did not God make every thing which has life keep the Sabbath? The birds fly about in the air on the Sabbath-day, and the lambs skip about in the field. Why does not God make the birds, and the lambs, and every thing which has life, keep the Sabbath?

Mrs. M. Every thing which has life does not need the Sabbath, perhaps. In trees and vegetables there are veins which carry the sap from the roots to the branches and leaves, and then back again to the roots, as blood is carried from the heart to every part of our bodies, and then back again, by arteries and veins. I suppose God might have made trees and vegetables, so that they would need to rest one day in seven, as we do. And I suppose God might have made the beasts that rove about in the woods, and the birds that fly about in the air, so that they would need the Sabbath as well as man. But he has not done it. The rose is never tired of hanging on the bush and being beautiful; nor the lily with standing on its stalk and being fragrant. The wild beasts of the forest, when undisturbed by man, never appear to be weary. They do not labor, they get their food, and then lie down to sleep. And the birds of the air, our Saviour says, " neither sow nor reap," have " neither storehouse nor barn " —so they are not anxious about laying up wealth, and getting a living, and are never tired by working.

Dr. Farre said further, that men who do not rest on the Sabbath may hold out longer than beasts of burden, but at last they will break down more suddenly. This want of rest on the Sabbath, would shorten their life and make them feebler in old age. He said it is a duty to keep the Sabbath, if it is a duty to preserve life. The committee asked him if he would recommend to every body who must work six days, to rest on the seventh? He said he would, and that *in the course of life they would gain by it.* He said he found it necessary for himself to work, as little as he could on the Sabbath; and that he has known many physicians and clergymen shorten their lives, because they had to labor six days in the week, without resting on the Sabbath.

Charles. Is this the reason that father always tries to go to meeting on the Sabbath?

Mrs. M. Your father never wishes to have any one send for him on the Sabbath unless it is necessary, as he wants the Sabbath for rest. And he says that our minister, who cannot rest on the Sabbath, ought to rest on Monday. And he tells our neighbors that they ought not to call upon the minister on Monday, if they can make their visits on any other day.

Do you think now, George, that the Sabbath is fitted for man, as the light is for the eye?

George. Yes, mother, it seems so to me, and I hope I shall be very thankful that the same kind Being who has given me eyes to see the light, has also let me live where I can rest my body one day in seven.

But, mother, uncle John said that it might do well enough for the rich, and for those who can afford it, to keep the Sabbath, but that for poor men and day laborers it is a heavy burden.

Mrs. M. Is it a burden, George, to have one's body made more vigorous?

George. No, mother.

Mrs. M. Or to have one's health better?

George. No, mother.

Mrs. M. Or to have one's life lengthened?

George. Certainly not, mother.

Mrs. M. But the distinguished medical men whose opinions I have quoted, say that all these things come from keeping the Sabbath.

George. But, mother, uncle John said that poor laboring men have to give up fifty-two days in a year on account of the Sabbath. The pay for these fifty-two days, he said, they could ill afford to lose. Add it to what they get now, and they might be very comfortable.

Mrs. M. Can people always get the same price for their labor?

George. No, mother; sometimes father has to give more for a day's work than he gives at other times.

Mrs. M. Why is this?

George. I never thought much about it, but I suppose it is because sometimes there are more laborers than work to be done. The more laborers there are the less wages they will get. When there is but little corn, the farmers ask more for it. And when you sent me to the grocer's, the other day, to get some oil, he told me that I must give him more than I gave the last time, because oil was growing scarce, and there was not much of it in market.

Mrs. M. Well, my son, suppose there were in a town three hundred and thirteen laborers. If you were to add fifty-two to their number, what change do you think there would be in the price of labor?

George. I suppose, mother, that labor might be one-sixth cheaper, if there was no more labor wanted than there is now, and all the new laborers were to be employed.

Mrs. M. I think there would be some such change. Now, George, suppose every body was to think as your uncle John does, that it is a burden for the poor to keep the Sabbath, and all should agree that the poor might work seven days in the week, instead of six. Do you not see that it would be just the same as if one-sixth part was added to the present number of laborers? Many farmers and manufacturers, who now employ seven men, would dismiss one of them; or else they would reduce their pay, and give them no more for seven days than they had given them for six.

George. It is so, mother.

Mrs. M. The poor man would labor fifty-two days more in a year than he does now; but he would get only the same amount of wages which he gets at present, while he rests on every one of these fifty-two days.

What do you think of the matter now, my son? Is it a burden for the poor to rest on the Sabbath?

George. O no, mother, the Sabbath is the poor man's friend.

Mrs. M. Yes, George, and one of the best friends which he has in the world. I have seen some rich people, who seem scarcely to know how to loiter away the hours during the six days, while poor men are hard at work, and I have thought what a burden these rich, idle people would consider the Sabbath. But when I have seen a poor man returning to his home as the sun is setting on Saturday night, I have wished to go and kneel down with him at his happy fireside, and join with him in thanks to God that another Sabbath has come, and the weary may once more find rest. O, my children, the Sabbath is the friend of every body, but it is especially the friend of the poor. They wrong their own souls—they wrong their own bodies, when they despise or think lightly of the Sabbath.

George. Mother, did the heathen at the Sandwich

Islands keep the Sabbath when our missionaries first went to live among them?

Mrs. M. No, my child.

George. Well, then, mother, were the poor any better off there than in countries where the Sabbath is kept strictly?

Mrs. M. No, my child. You can scarcely find a man in our land who has not a better house to live in, and more comforts, than most of the chiefs had in the Sandwich Islands. As to the poor in those islands, they have no property. The chiefs own every thing, and take just as much as they please of what the poor raise from the land. The poor there are more miserable than you can imagine.

George. Would it not be better for them to have the Sabbath?

Mrs. M. The Sabbath might do as much for them as it has done for the United States.

We should have been worshiping Woden and Thor with our Saxon forefathers, but for the Sabbath; just as the Sandwich Islanders worshiped gods of wood and stone. It is the Sabbath that makes the people of the United States industrious and comfortable; for we do not naturally love to work, any more than the Sandwich Islanders; and we should not work more than was absolutely necessary if the rich took our property away whenever they please. *The only reason, George, why the people in this country are not as wretched as the people were in the Sandwich Islands, is that we have the Gospel and they had it not.*

The Gospel has given us good laws to guard our property when we get it, and so we have some encouragement to work. The Sandwich Islanders were without good laws, because they were without the Gospel. But no nation can have the Gospel and good laws without the Sabbath. You might as well look for rain without clouds. If your uncle John says again that it is a burden to the poor to keep the Sabbath, ask him to tell you why the people of the Sandwich Islands are so poor?

I have been anxious to show you, this evening, as clearly as I am able, the use of the Sabbath in refreshing the weary bodies of laboring men and beasts; for some persons, who deny that the Sabbath was instituted by God, if they will not keep it as he commands, may at least be restrained by such a motive from disturbing the rest of others. Still, as I shall show you before we close our conversations, mere rest is not the highest use of the Sabbath. To those that observe it aright, it is the emblem and pledge of a more glorious rest. Never forget this, my children. Never let the shadows of Saturday evening gather around you, without thinking of the rest and peace of heaven. I never feel so near to another world, and so much as if time was melting into eternity, as when the sun, at

SABBATH NECESSARY FOR THE BODY.

the close of the week, setting behind the western hills, reminds me that another Sabbath is coming to release my hands and thoughts from the objects of earth, and to welcome my spirit home to God. Do you remember, George, the lines on "*Saturday Evening*" which I gave you a few weeks ago?

George.

> " Sweet is the last, the parting ray,
>   " That ushers placid evening in;
> " When, with the still, expiring day,
>   " The Sabbath's peaceful hours begin.
> " How grateful to the anxious breast
> " The sacred hours of holy rest!
>
> " Hush'd is the tumult of the day,
>   " And worldly cares and business cease;
> " While soft the vesper breezes play,
>   " To hymn the glad return of peace.
> " Delightful season! kindly given
> " To turn the wandering thoughts to heaven.
>
> • Oft as this peaceful hour shall come,
>   " Lord, raise my thoughts from earthly things
> " And bear them to my heavenly home,
>   " On faith and hope's celestial wings,
> " Till the last gleam of life decay,
> " In one eternal Sabbath-day!"

EVENING VII.

SABBATH NECESSARY FOR THE MIND.

Mrs. M. My dear children, last Sabbath evening we saw how *admirably fitted the Sabbath is to the human body. Now let us see if it is as well fitted to the human mind.*

I think you told me, George, that your vacation is to begin next Wednesday, and last a fortnight?

George. Yes, mother, and I am glad of it; for I am almost tired of studying, and wish to rest for a while.

Mrs. M. Perhaps your uncle John would consider this a useless waste of time.

George. If he were as young as he was once, and as I am now, I do not believe he would think so. Do you think our vacation is a useless waste of time, mother?

Mrs. M. No, my son. I have always noticed that you love to study better, and make more progress after vacation than before. The mind, so long as it is connected with the body, must have seasons for resting. I know some people wonder how any one can be tired who has nothing to do but sit still and study. But the mind tires as well as the body; or rather, I ought to say, the brain gets tired of thinking, as much as the arms get tired of working. I suppose angels are never tired; and when we get a spiritual body we shall not, perhaps, ever become weary by thinking and feeling.

Hard and long study, so physicians tell us, excites the brain and makes the blood flow to it more rapidly, and in larger quantity than at other times. The brain becomes heated, and the head often feels full and pressed. The blood inclines to rush to the brain constantly, and, if care is not taken in season, the man may become insane, and at last be a confirmed maniac. He did not stop thinking so soon as he ought. Perhaps he did not stop on the Sabbath, but kept thinking about his studies as on other days.

I read, not long since, in the life of Sir Isaac Newton, how he discovered the law of gravitation, or what makes all bodies, when thrown up into the air, fall to the ground, and what binds the moon to the earth, and the earth to the sun, and all parts of the world together. He had been thinking and studying hard a good while, and wishing very much to find out what made the apple fall to the ground, as he lay under an apple-tree in his garden. When he began to be almost sure that he should discover what he was seeking, he was so agitated and became so nervous that he durst not go on with his study. He gave his papers to a friend and told him to complete the calculations. If he had not diverted his mind, he would, very likely, have lost his reason.

Now we see how well fitted the Sabbath is to the nature of the mind. The brain calls for repose, and cannot long be kept in a healthy state without it. The Sabbath gives just the repose which the brain calls for, and so much needs. Light is no better fitted to the eye than the repose of the Sabbath is to the nature of the mind, or, as I might say, to the wants of the brain. For learned men, who have examined the subject, say that the mind makes use of the brain for thinking, just as it makes use of the limbs for walking, and of the arms for hammering the iron on the anvil.

The mind not only *thinks, but feels.* And the influence of deep feeling on the mind, when long continued, is often very great and unhappy. It is no uncommon thing for deep-settled grief to overpower the reason and make persons insane. You remember that when our neighbor Mrs. F. had lost her dear little Frederick, she was very melancholy, and her friends were afraid she would become deranged. So her husband went with her on a long journey, that she might see a great many new things, and sometimes forget her dear boy who was dead. They knew that if she stayed at home she would be thinking of him all the while, and this might at last make her insane. They did not wish her to be thinking about her loss all the time. So her husband tried to divert her mind on the journey as much as he could. He pointed out to her every thing beautiful and strange that he saw. By and by she took some notice of what he showed her, and then she began to recover from her grief.

One of the uses of the Sabbath, my children, is to divert the mind from its cares, and business, and sorrows, and thus to keep it in a healthy state.

In the worship of God's house we forget our sorrow. While we think of the mansions where there is no grief, and no disappointment, our burden is thrown off, and our sinking hearts are refreshed. To be sure, cares will come again, and the clouds of sorrow will again overshadow us, but another Sabbath will scatter them all away. In this manner the Sabbath diverts the mind, just as the new objects on the journey diverted and soothed the mind of Mrs. F.

I happen to think of a very striking fact or two, which will illustrate what I have said. A few years ago the Marquis of Londonderry killed himself, in what was supposed to be a state of mental derangement. He was the chief of those whom the king trusted to manage the government, and was called the Prime Minister. He did not keep the Sabbath. He let the business and the cares of the week perplex his mind during the Sabbath, just as on other days. He never laid down his burden. It was more than he could carry without resting, and at last he sunk under its weight.

I cannot tell what would have happened if he had remembered "the Sabbath day to keep it holy;" but I think it very probable that if he had gone to church on the Sabbath, instead of going to his office, his life and reason might have continued a good while longer. If he had attended public worship, while listening to so eloquent a man as Dr. Chalmers, or joining in the prayers and praises of the house of God, I suppose he could not have thought of his business. He would have forgotten the duties and cares of the Prime Minister; and would have been refreshed and cheered by the services of the Sabbath. When the day of rest was over, he could enter again upon the business of the week with new energy and spirit. His body would be more active, his mind more calm, and his judgment more clear and sound. Dr. Farre, in the examination which I have already mentioned, said that he had known many senators and others in the higher ranks, destroy their lives by continually thinking, and not resting on the Sabbath.

You have often heard of Mr. Wilberforce, the friend of Africa and the slaves. He was a statesman as well as a christian. During one part of his life, he had to do a great deal of public business. But let him be ever so much occupied, he always observed the Sabbath. He says he should have sunk under the weight of his labor, if he had not thrown it off one day in seven. He could not have borne to think so much without resting. He says that several of his associates in public life died early of disease, or became insane and committed suicide, who, if they had kept the Sabbath, might have been vigorous and active many years longer.

The Sabbath is equally well fitted to aid men in *judging correctly*. When we form a judgment, you know, we compare things together. If I wished to determine which of two apples is the larger, I should place them side by side, that is, I should compare one with the other, and then judge or form my opinion. You have often seen your father's glass, which makes things appear larger than they really are.

Susan. O yes, mother, and how large and beautiful the butterfly's wing looked, which you let us see through the glass last summer.

Mrs. M. Now, if, in deciding which apple is the larger, I were to look at one of them with the naked eye, and at the other through the magnifying glass, do you think, George, I should judge correctly?

George. I suppose you might not, mother; and though I always think what you say is right, I should be almost afraid you had been deceived, and judged wrong about the apple.

Mrs. M. When men think of any object a great while without interruption, it appears larger and of more importance than it really is. This continued thinking has the same effect on the mind which looking through a magnifying glass has on the eye. Now suppose men want to judge between this object, of which they have been thinking so long, and some other object. They will be in danger of judging wrong, just as I was in the case of the apple; because one object appears to them to be larger than it really is, and the other does not. Now, George, what would you do to make them judge correctly, in this case?

George. Why, mother, I think the best way would be to tell them to think of something else, a day or two before they form their judgment.

Mrs. M. You could not give them better advice, my son. And this is just the use of the Sabbath, in helping men to judge correctly, and in saving them from judging wrong. In this way, I have no doubt, the Sabbath has prevented many a bad bargain. Some object, of which men have thought too long, becomes, in their view, larger than it is,—they value it more highly than they ought, and they would be more likely to give more for it than it is worth. But the Sabbath comes; they read their Bibles, they attend public worship, they think of the endless Sabbath, and forget what they have been thinking of during the week. And when they return to their business on Monday, they find out their mistake. The Sabbath, I might say, removes the magnifying glass from their eyes, and now they see just how large the object is. This will keep them from judging wrong, and getting into difficulty. I think a cautious man would wish to rest over the Sabbath, when his feelings have been much excited, before he ventures to judge in any case.

I have now shown you, my children, that the Sabbath is fitted to the *bodies* of men, or their *physical* nature; and to their *minds*, or their *intellectual* nature. Is it as well fitted to their *moral* nature? Will it help men to love and serve God? Will it help them to prepare for another world?

This, my children, is the great use of the Sabbath. For of how little worth are our bodies if we compare them with our immortal souls? What if, by resting on the Sabbath, we live a little longer, and enjoy a little better health, and are a little more vigorous and free from pain? The body will die at last, after all our care. And what if the Sabbath helps us to think, without losing the command of our mind, and becoming insane? And what if it helps us to bear our sorrows and our misfortunes, and makes us more cheerful and happy? And what if it improves our judgment, and saves us from making injudicious bargains? Whether we are happy here, or wretched, this life will soon be over. But the life to come will never end. The soul will never die.

Now, is the Sabbath fitted to aid man in preparing for the future world? Is it as necessary for his moral nature, as light is to the eye, or as food is to the body?

There can be no doubt that it is. Man cannot open his eyes and look at heaven and the objects of the spiritual world, as he can look at the cities, and mountains, and rivers of earth. But though man cannot see these objects, he must often think of them, or it will be of no use that they are spoken of in the Bible. And he will not think of them as much as he ought, unless he has more time than most persons suppose they can spare from their daily business. He must, too, think of these objects sometimes a good while, or they will not make much impression on his mind. Now the Sabbath is just such a season as man needs, for thinking, without interruption, about the things revealed in the Bible. It is a kind of school, in which we can spend one day every week in studying the character of God, his works, and government, and the redemption of man through our Lord Jesus Christ. And who would not wish to belong to this school? What lessons are taught! What rewards are offered! What pleasures enjoyed! If children are foolish, that had rather be ignorant than go to school where those things chiefly are taught which fit men to be useful and happy in the present world; how much more foolish are those persons who dislike this school of the Sabbath, where, through the blessing of God, they might prepare for a crown of glory that fadeth not away!

Where the Sabbath is not observed, you will find that men think and care very little about another world. They live as if they expected to live always on earth. They forget God, when they forget the Sabbath; they forget Jesus Christ and his salvation when they forget the Lord's day.

Men will not be prayerful, and devoted, and pious, where they neglect the Sabbath. They must have time for meditation, time for prayer, time for reading the Bible, time for worshiping God in his sanctuary, or they will lose all their religious feeling. They must stop their worldly business one day in seven, or their moral nature will suffer as much as their bodies will suffer for want of the Sabbath. They are in no more danger of becoming insane from constant thinking, than they are of becoming worldly by constant attention to business. In both cases, they must stop; they must keep the Sabbath, or the mind will get into a bad and dangerous state.

Like a neglected garden, where the tall weeds spring up and overshadow the flowers, so would the heart be without the Sabbath. The rank weeds of worldliness and care would choke the growth of piety. But the Sabbath comes, like Adam into Eden, to dress and to keep the garden of the soul. It clears away the weeds of worldliness and care. Then the flowers of devotion expand to the light of the Sun of Righteousness, and drink in the refreshing dews of heaven. They scatter their fragrance on every breeze, and unfold their beauty to every eye.

On other days, laborers, servants, and domestics are often so much pressed by those who employ them, that it is very difficult for them to attend properly to the wants of the soul. Some persons are tempted to neglect secret prayer and reading the Bible, because they wish to be about their worldly business. Or they hurry through these duties so as to do them very little good. But on the Sabbath they cannot work on their farms or in their shops; they cannot make bargains or seek after office. Men, therefore, are not driven by necessity, and they have no temptation from their worldly concerns, to neglect secret prayer and reading the Bible on the Sabbath.

And if there was no Sabbath, too, men would not assemble every week for the worship of God. But public worship awakens the sympathies of men. The cold heart of one is kindled into a flame by the zeal and devotion of another. Feeling flows from soul to soul, just as when men gather to celebrate some joyful festival. How well suited, then, are the Sabbath and its services to the moral nature and condition of man!

Charles. I do not see, mother, that I need a day of rest so often as the Sabbath comes.

Mrs. M. You do not have to labor so hard now as you may have to labor if you live to be a man.

But I think, Charles, if you had to get up as soon as it is light, and work ten or twelve hours every day, as boys no older than you do in England, you would count the days to the Sabbath, just as you was this evening counting the weeks to Thanksgiving.

Charles. Would these little boys have to work so hard every day all the year if there was no Sabbath?

Mrs. M. I suppose so, my son.

Charles. O mother, I am very glad God made the Sabbath for these poor children, so that they can rest when they are tired. I hope I shall never wish again there was not any Sabbath, as I used to wish when I wanted to play with my wooden horse, and you would tell me I must not play, for it was the Sabbath.

Susan. I never get so tired of thinking, mother, that I need any Sabbath.

Mrs. M. No, Susan; little girls like you do not often become insane by thinking too long on one thing.

Susan. And I do not see, mother, what need there is of the Sabbath to help people bear their cares and sorrows.

Mrs. M. You are young, my child, and know very little what cares and sorrows mean. You do not feel so much now as you will when you grow older, how kind God is in giving us the repose of the Sabbath.

It is very dark and rainy to-night. You sit here in a pleasant room, with a bright light and comfortable fire, and wonder what need people ever have of the moon and the stars. But you will not wonder when you have been tossed over the waves, as some poor sailor, perhaps, is tossing to-night, without moon or stars to guide your course, while the wind whistles through the rigging, and you are afraid every moment that the vessel will dash against the rocks.

But, my child, though you may not now need one day in seven to rest your body, or refresh your mind, you need the Sabbath to make you think about God and prepare for heaven. The Bible tells us there remaineth a rest to the people of God. This rest, my child, is in heaven. It is sweet, unbroken, and eternal. None who enjoy it think it a weariness, and happy are they who shall enjoy it for ever. But it remaineth *only to the people of God.* Think of this, my child. You know you cannot be one of God's people without a new heart. You must, then, have a new heart before you die, or you will not spend this delightful, unending Sabbath, with the people of God.

Before we separate, you may repeat, Susan, that charming hymn which I taught you about the eternal Sabbath.

Susan.

> Thine earthly Sabbaths, Lord, we love;
> But there's a nobler rest above;
> To that our longing souls aspire,
> With ardent pangs of strong desire.
>
> No more fatigue, no more distress,
> Nor sin nor hell shall reach the place;
> No groans to mingle with the songs
> That warble from immortal tongues.
>
> No rude alarms of raging foes;
> No cares to break the long repose;
> No midnight shade, no clouded sun,
> But sacred, high, eternal noon.
>
> Around thy throne grant we may meet,
> And give us but the lowest seat,
> We'll shout thy praise and join the song
> Of the triumphant, holy throng.

EVENING VIII.

SABBATH NECESSARY FOR SOCIETY.

Uncle John told me, mother, last week, said George, that there ought to be no laws to compel men to keep the Sabbath. He said all ought to do as they please about observing it. If they choose to rest, very well; and if they do not choose to rest, it is no one's business.

Mrs. M. Does your uncle John think it right to make laws that no one shall commit murder, or steal, or be guilty of perjury?

George. He must think such laws would be right.

Mrs. M. Why would it be right to make laws against murder, theft, and perjury?

George. Because men could not live together without such laws.

Mrs. M. You mean that these laws are fitted to the condition of man in society, and that this is a reason why they should be made, *even if God had not forbidden men to murder, and steal, and lie.*

George. Yes, mother.

Mrs. M. If the Sabbath, then, is fitted to the condition of men living together in the same neighborhood, town, or state, would it not be right to make laws requiring them to keep the Sabbath?

George. I do not see, mother, why it would not be as right as it is to make laws against murder, and theft, and perjury.

Mrs. M. The Sabbath is fitted to promote the welfare of society.

This is the reason why, in almost all christian countries, laws have been made to secure it from violation. These laws are not made merely because

God has sanctified the Sabbath, but because such laws are of as much use to society as laws that forbid murder, theft, and perjury.

George. I wish, mother, you would show that the Sabbath *is fitted* to promote the welfare of society; for uncle John says, the Sabbath often does society a great deal of hurt. He says when men are idle, and have nothing to do, they are much more likely to get into mischief than when they are busy at work. He says that laboring men often spend on the Sabbath, in amusement and in drinking, all they earn during the week, and leave their families to suffer, if not to starve. He says it would be much better for them to work on the Sabbath, than to be idle and spend all they earn, and get sick or wounded from their frolics on that day.

Mrs. M. Are not most of the crimes which we hear and read of committed in the night?

George. Yes, mother.

Mrs. M. The apostle calls these crimes the works of darkness. But because some men who ought to be asleep, spend the night in doing mischief, would you have no night in which men could repose? And because some men abuse the Sabbath, and do what God forbids, would you not have any Sabbath? If God had commanded men to frolic on the Sabbath, to spend the day in gambling, and drinking, and dancing, and fighting, your uncle John might say, with more reason, that men had better work on the Sabbath. But God commands men to rest, and keep the Sabbath holy. It is not the Sabbath, which God has sanctified, that does so much mischief, but the Sabbath as kept by wicked men. We have no right to profane the Sabbath, and pervert it to wrong uses, and then complain that it does much injury, and say that we could do better without it.

The Sabbath, which I shall try to show you promotes the welfare of society, is a day of rest from our common business; a day devoted to the worship of God, to public and private instruction, to religious reading and meditation, and to works of kindness and mercy. These duties are all interwoven in the Sabbath; or rather, I might say, make a part of it. I agree with Dr. Rush, that "amusements of every kind, on the Sabbath, beget habits of idleness and a love of pleasure, which extend their influence to every day of the week." I condemn them utterly, and as heartily as your uncle John. Better have no Sabbath, than spend it in dissipation and amusement.

The original meaning of the Sabbath is *rest from labor*. As a *day of repose*, the Sabbath is of great use in promoting *order and good morals* in society.

You remember, George, that you read to me, a few evenings ago, from Russel's History of Modern Europe, an account of the Truce of God, in the eleventh or twelfth century.

George. Yes, mother, and you told me it was a sort of Sabbath, and if men had only kept this truce, it would have been very useful in preventing mischief.

Charles. What is the "Truce of God," which brother George read about in that book you mentioned?

Mrs. M. Many centuries ago, all the nobles and great men in Europe claimed the right of going to war with each other whenever they pleased. This was called the right of private war. You know that only kings and governments are permitted to declare war now, and the wars which they make are called public wars. The Arabs still go to war with each other, and any one else, as often as they choose, and they are not punished for it, because it is the custom of their country.

These private wars had become so troublesome and dangerous, that the governments of several countries in Europe, about seven or eight hundred years ago, tried to put an end to them. But men love to fight so well, that the governments could not stop the nobles from going to war, whenever one thought another had insulted him, or done him an injury.

Men at that day were very ignorant, and very superstitious. It was therefore thought best to try what superstition could do in stopping these private wars. So it was pretended that a letter had been sent from heaven to a bishop of Aquitane, in France, which commanded all men to cease quarrelling, and to make peace with each other. From some cause, the historian does not say what, men were suffering great calamities when this pretended command was given. I suppose there may have been a destructive pestilence, such as now and then swept over countries in former times. Or there may have been a famine, such as often prevailed before men understood agriculture as well as they do now, and when there was not much intercourse among different nations.

But whatever was the cause, they were in great trouble. So they were very ready to do what they supposed was commanded from heaven. They hoped that God would not, then, be angry with them and punish them any longer. There was a general reconciliation. Men that had always been bitter enemies, and fought whenever they met, now came together as friends. A rule was made that no man should attack or injure his foes during the holidays of the church, and from every Thursday evening to the next Monday morning. The days between Thursday and Monday were to be regarded as holy, because our Saviour died on Friday and rose on Sunday. This ceasing from fighting, during these days, was called "*the Truce of God.*" If this truce had been kept strictly, the historian says, there would have been so much time for men's passions to cool, that it would have gone far towards putting an end to private wars.

In the same way the Sabbath gives the minds of men a season of repose and reflection. Their passions get cool, and they do not any longer wish to injure one another. This is the reason why I told George that the "Truce of God," which he was reading about, is somewhat like the Sabbath.

When men are very angry and violent, if you can only persuade them to stop and reflect a moment, they become calm, and their anger dies away. I think there would not be many law-suits for assault and battery, if men would always wait half an hour after they raise their arm to strike, before they give the blow. They would soon see how foolish it is to be angry, and to wish to take revenge for an insult or injury.

When hurried by business, or excited by party feeling, men often do things for which they feel very sorry as soon as they have time to reflect. Such a season is given by the Sabbath.

Temptation blinds the mind during the cares and business of the week. It threatens to overpower us and lead us into sin. But amid the repose of the Sabbath, the judgment is clear, and the conscience is active, and eternity is nigh. Then we see how temptation is trying to deceive and destroy our souls, and we escape from its snare.

Men are often prone to prize wealth too highly,

and may be in danger of doing wrong to obtain it. Perhaps they begin to think of some scheme for getting what belongs to another, by dishonesty and fraud. But they dare not meditate on the scheme on the Sabbath. In these quiet and solemn hours the mind becomes ashamed of the plan for defrauding a neighbor, and it is laid aside before its execution is begun.

The Sabbath places a wall between the angry man and the object of his anger; between the revengeful man and the object of his fury; between the covetous man and the object of his desire; between the ambitious man and the office at which he aims. It brings them all to a stand. It bids them pause and reflect. It changes the tempest into a healthful breeze—the raging tide into a murmuring ripple.

The voice of the Sabbath is a voice of gentleness. I have sometimes thought that even the music of the birds is softer on the Sabbath than on other days; and that the echoes in the fields and in the groves are more melodious and soothing. To the rudeness of the passionate, and to the clamorous desires of the greedy and ambitious, the Sabbath speaks, in the language of Him who calmed the winds and the waves, "Peace, be still."

The Sabbath is admirably fitted to *promote intelligence in the community.*

If there was no Sabbath, there would be no

ministers settled over congregations, as there are now. And if there were no ministers, especially in country towns, there would be few good schools. Clergymen are almost always on the committees for examining teachers, and for visiting schools. And schools, when neglected by clergymen, are not often flourishing.

Think, too, my children, how much knowledge must be collected, in the course of a long life, by devoting a part of one day in seven to reading and reflection! Good deacon Stockton knows much more than the father of Thomas Bradish. The difference would not be much greater if deacon Stockton had gone to school one half of each seventh day, from his childhood until the age of threescore years and ten; while the father of Thomas Bradish had never gone to school a day in his life. But a great part of this difference, I have no doubt, is owing to the different manner in which they keep the Sabbath. The father of Thomas Bradish goes to hunting and fishing on the Sabbath, or else he roves about the fields, or spends the day in sleep. But deacon Stockton, who owns a share in the parish library, is always careful to have some good book to read on the Sabbath. To be sure, he says there is no book like the Bible; still he thinks it best to spend a part of the Sabbath in reading other books. You can scarcely name a biography of good men and women which deacon Stockton has not read. He is well acquainted with history and chronology. He knows all about the countries where the missionaries reside. He works hard during the week, and has a large family to support; but yet he finds time, by keeping the Sabbath strictly, to grow in knowledge, as well as in grace.

There are many such men as deacon Stockton in almost every congregation where the Sabbath is observed—venerable men, men of principle and good sense, who are made so, very much, by keeping the Sabbath.

Now converse with the father of Thomas Bradish. When young, he was a schoolmate of deacon Stockton, and was the brighter, I have been told, of the two. But the father of Thomas Bradish did not love to keep the Sabbath. While deacon Stockton was reading on the Sabbath, he was hunting, or fishing, or haunting the tavern. And now you would scarcely think he knows how to read; for if you ask him any question about history, or about the places where the missionaries live, or about any of the biographies of good men, you will find him as ignorant almost as a child. I suppose he does not even know that there ever was such a man as Henry Martyn or John Newton.

Mrs. Hannah More, whom we read about last week, says she used to read a great many religious books on the Sabbath. She says she read Lowth, and Atterbury, and Warburton, and Baxter, and Doddridge, and Jeremy Taylor, and many more.

Beside the knowledge gained on the Sabbath by reading, much is gained from attendance on preaching. I have heard it said that the taste of a people is often like that of their pastor. I see no reason why this should not be so, as well as that the taste of George, and Charles, and Susan should resemble that of their father or mother. What we hear or see often, we are very apt to imitate. And I have no doubt that people will imitate, more or less, the manners and tones of voice, and expressions of their minister, as really as that children will imitate these same things in their parents.

I have seen the statement that you could distinguish the members of a certain parish, where there had not been any minister for a great many years, by the tones of their voice and the manner of their pronunciation.

Think, too, how it will sharpen the intellect, to listen so often to sermons which are well arranged, and full of sound and logical argument. I love to look at the house of worship, as a place where the mind is strengthened and disciplined by the same services which purify the heart and fit the soul for heaven. It is a common school. From this school none need be excluded. The poor and the rich are all in the same class—are all taught the same lesson, and may all make the same progress. We shall see the value of this school, if we reflect that in some countries a large part of the people have no opportunity of getting knowledge, except on the Sabbath.

EVENING IX.

SABBATH NECESSARY FOR SOCIETY.

Mrs. M. I began to show you, my dear children, in our last conversation, that the *Sabbath is fitted to promote intelligence in the community.* We will converse about the same subject a few minutes this evening.

There would be no Sabbath-schools without the Sabbath. Children go to these schools chiefly to learn their duty to God and the way to heaven. But besides this, the scholars learn a great deal about the history, geography, and manners and customs of ancient nations mentioned in the Bible.

Many children, even in this country, would never know how to read, if they were not taught in a Sabbath-school. Their parents feel unable to clothe them and send them to the common schools—or else they are ignorant, and do not know the value of knowledge. These unfortunate children often live far away from villages and churches, in poor cottages on the mountains, or in the distant valleys. But they are sought out by the kind and benevolent teacher. They are clothed, they are supplied with books, they are taught to read, and they soon feel that they may become respectable and useful.

I know a young lady who watches the children and youth in the galleries of the church, to see if there are any that do not go to the Sabbath-school. When she notices any such, she finds out their names, and invites them to join the school. Not long ago, she found in this way a female seventeen or eighteen years old, who could not read even a letter. She persuaded her to go to the Sabbath-school, and promised to give her a Bible. For a few weeks, the family with whom the scholar lived were obliged to read the lesson to her, and she remembered as much of it as she could. But she was so anxious to learn the lesson without aid, that she studied diligently, and before a great while, could read a chapter in the Bible very well. And then she could read the books in the Sabbath-school library; for the poor can get books from the Sabbath-school libraries, which are useful and profitable to read during the week, as well as to study on the Sabbath.

In this, and in many other ways, the Sabbath

tends to level the distinctions among men. It tends to unite the rich and the poor. It tends to keep the rich from being proud and insolent, and the poor from being ignorant, and from hating the rich. It binds society together in love and harmony.

There are many such cases in this country as that I have just mentioned, and more, I suppose, in England and Ireland. Not many years ago, a ragged, ignorant, wicked boy was wandering about the streets of London on the Sabbath. He was persuaded, by some kind teacher, to go to the Sabbath-school. At first he was not a very promising scholar, but the teacher was patient. I suppose the teacher remembered that God bears long with us all, and does not quickly cast us off as though we should never become any better. Young Milne, for that was his name, at last began to love his lesson, then he began to love his Saviour, and soon he began to love the heathen. He wanted to do them good, and to teach them to love the Saviour, and be fitted for heaven. So he went to China, and afterwards to Malacca, and was one of the most devoted and successful missionaries in modern times.

Charles. I think, mother, the books in the Sabbath-school library are very interesting, and I love to read them very much.

Mrs. M. There were but few such books when I was at your age, Charles. I should have been very glad to get almost any of the excellent little books which you bring home from the Sabbath-school. I knew scarcely any thing about the geography of the Bible when I was young. I used to read about Jerusalem, and Samaria, and Gaza, and Beer-sheba, but I did not know where these places were situated. I knew they were somewhere in Asia, but I could not point them out on the map, as Susan can. Indeed, I did not have any map to show the situation of places mentioned in the Bible; and I suppose I might never have had any, but for the American Sunday-school Union. I fear, my children, that you will not value as you ought the privileges you enjoy, because they are so many, and so easy to be obtained.

Susan. Did you not always know, mother, where Jerusalem is? I am sure I always knew; for I cannot remember when I did not know where it is.

Mrs. M. Think, my child, of what the Bible says, "Unto whomsoever much is given, of them much will be required."

But men must be *governed* as well as educated. And the Sabbath is fitted to aid in governing men who live together in society. If they cast off the fear of God and love to one another, and are not willing to do what is right, how will you govern them?

Charles. I would make laws, and then threaten to punish them severely if they broke the laws.

Mrs. M. You cannot govern men in this way, if they do not fear God and love one another, and are not willing to do what is right. They hope you will not find out when they do wrong,—for the laws cannot see, and you who make the laws are not always present. They can do wrong when you are asleep, or when you are absent, or when the world is covered with night.

And if you think they have done wrong, they must be tried before you can punish them. And they hope they shall be able to bribe the witnesses, or deceive the judges and the jury. They always hope, in some way, to escape punishment if they break the laws.

Charles. Well, then, if I could not govern men by laws, I would try to govern them by armies.

Mrs. M. You collect a large military force, I will suppose. All over your kingdom are officers in their military dress, and soldiers with their swords and bayonets. But you cannot govern men so, when they cease to fear God, and to love one another, and to be willing to do what is right. France tried it, but she did not succeed. She declared there is no God, and no hereafter, and that death is an eternal sleep. She said there should be no Sabbath, and she attempted to blot it out. And then men began to murder one another, and to hate one another, and to commit all manner of wickedness. Millions, I suppose, were killed in a very few years. No one was safe, man, woman, or child. There was no fear of God in the land, so it was full of murder, and theft, and perjury. At length they were obliged to have a Sabbath, one day in ten, and to own that there is a God. They had finally to return to their old practice, and keep one day in seven. You cannot govern men who live together in society, by military force, without the fear of God, and the love of one another, and a willingness to do what is right.

Charles. I do not know how I could govern them, then, mother.

Mrs. M. See, now, how easily men can be governed, when there is a Sabbath to make them fear God and his law. They learn that God is every where—that he seeth through the thick darkness, that they cannot escape the notice of his eye, and that in the court where they will hereafter be tried, they can neither deceive nor bribe the judge. They are told this, from Sabbath to Sabbath, in their childhood; they are told it in their youth; they are told it in manhood; they are told it in old age. When the heart is softened by prayer and praise in God's house, they are charged, by the joys of heaven and by the pains of hell, to avoid sin and obey the laws.

Do you think we could live happily together, if George was not kind to his brother Charles, and to his sister Susan; and if Charles and Susan were not grateful to their parents, and if your father and I did not love you all? But human laws cannot make George kind, nor Charles and Susan grateful, nor your parents affectionate. There are a great many more such things, without which men could not live happily together, that human laws could no more make men do, than they can bind the sun. You may persuade men to be courteous, and temperate, and industrious, and forgiving, by what the Bible tells them, on the Sabbath, but you cannot force them to be so by human laws.

All the wicked deeds which men commit, come forth from the heart. But human laws cannot look into the heart, and see what is passing there. Murder may live in the heart many years, but human laws will not know it, and cannot prevent it. Fraud may lay his plans there month after month, but human laws cannot stop his work. Envy may sit and pine away in the heart, and ambition may form schemes of treason there without any check from human laws. Men may chase the lion to his den, but they cannot enter in and slay him.

But the law of God searches every hiding-place of the heart. It breaks up the plans of guilt. It drives forth every thing impure from the soul, as the money-changers were driven from the temple. Human laws only try to purify the streams, but the law of God cleanses the fountain.

It is easy, therefore, you see, to govern men, when the Sabbath makes them fear God, and love one another, and willing to do what is right. How admirably fitted is the Sabbath to aid in governing men who live together in society!

George. I think, mother, that the people of the United States ought to regard the Sabbath more than any other nation.

Mrs. M. Why do you think the Sabbath ought to be so much regarded in the United States?

George. Because, mother, I have often read that *morality is the foundation of a republican government, and I think that the Sabbath promotes morality.*

Mrs. M. Without good morals a republic like ours cannot long exist. The French once tried to have a republican government, but they were too immoral, and their government lasted only a little while.

The Sabbath, as you say, promotes good morals, and so is fitted for a republican government. I suppose there is not a more moral country in the world than New England has been for two hundred years. And there is no country in the world where the Sabbath has been kept better than here. The Scotch are a very moral people; but the Scotch have kept the Sabbath more strictly than any other nation in Europe. In France, Spain, and Italy, the Sabbath is a day for shows and amusements—for visiting and military parade. New England and Scotland are far more moral than these countries. No nation in the world is moral and sober where the Sabbath is despised and trampled on, and made a day for mirth and sports. The committee of the British Parliament, before referred to, say, it appears in evidence, that in each trade, in proportion to its disregard of the Lord's day, is the immorality of those engaged in it. A Scotch writer says, that in 1763 his countrymen were decent, dignified, and delicate in their manners, but that in 1783 they were comparatively loose, dissipated, and licentious. One great reason for the change is, that in 1763 they kept the Sabbath much more strictly than in 1783.

Now let us look among those who break the laws and are punished, and see whether they were accustomed to keep the Sabbath. Scarcely a criminal is hung, who, if he says any thing about his wickedness, does not confess that it began by breaking the Sabbath. You remember, George, our visit to the state prison. There were almost two hundred prisoners. Some of them were old and gray-headed, and some of them were young and almost children. One boy was only a little older than Charles. I did not ask him whether his mother taught him to keep the Sabbath, but I think she did not.

Charles. I hope I never shall be put in the state prison, for my mother teaches me not to break the Sabbath.

Mrs. M. I hope you will not, Charles; but

remember what the Bible says, "Let him that thinketh he standeth take heed lest he fall;" and feel as a good man once did, when he said respecting himself, while a criminal was passing by to the gallows, "There, but for the grace of God, goes Richard Baxter."

But mothers cannot take a better course, if they wish to fit their children for the state prison and for the gallows, than to suffer them to violate the Sabbath. O how the heart of that little boy's mother must ache, if she ever sees him shut up at night alone in his dark cell.

The chaplain of the state prison, who talks with the prisoners, and learns all about their character, and what they have done, says that out of every *hundred* confined there, not far from *ninety* have been accustomed to disregard the Sabbath. At the Charlestown prison, in Massachusetts, out of *two hundred* and *fifty-six* prisoners, *one hundred* and *eighty* had lived in a general violation of the Sabbath. I suppose, therefore, that at least three-fourths of the criminals, or seventy-five in every hundred, who are hung, or sent to the state prisons in New-England, are habitual Sabbath breakers.

I think it will not be claimed that more than one person in ten in Connecticut might be properly called an habitual Sabbath-breaker. I do not suppose there is more than one in twenty or thirty. But allow that there is one in ten. Then the habitual Sabbath-breakers, in proportion to their number, ought to furnish one-tenth of the criminals, or ten in every hundred; whereas they furnish *seventy-five* in a *hundred*. This is more than seven times their proper share. Well might the learned Blackstone remark, that a corruption of morals usually follows a profanation of the Sabbath.

So you see that the Sabbath favors morality, and is, therefore, well fitted to a republican government, which cannot last long when the people cease to be virtuous. George said truly that the people of the United States ought to regard the Sabbath more than other nations regard it.

But there is another reason why our nation should be very anxious to preserve the Sabbath. I do not suppose that any of you have thought of it.

George. What is it, mother?

Mrs. M. There is not any other nation, I think, which has so good a Sabbath as we have in the United States. We have not received from our forefathers a French Sabbath, to spend in sport, and shows, and military reviews. Our Sabbath is a good old English Sabbath, or rather, I might say, a good old Puritan Sabbath, without the gloom which to some extent, perhaps, was given to it by our forefathers. I scarcely know whether a French Sabbath would be worth having. I think it might do almost as much harm as good.

And not only is our Sabbath better than any

other on earth, *but a better use can be made of it.* A larger part of our people can read the Bible, and understand it, than in most other countries. The Sabbath, too, will do good or hurt, according as the doctrines which are impressed upon the mind, on that day, are true or false. If our people were to go to the temple of idols, and burn sacrifices on the Sabbath, the day would be a curse to the nation. Or if they were to go to Mohammedan mosques, and worship there, the Sabbath would be of very little value. And were they to spend the day in Roman Catholic cathedrals, hearing prayers in a language they cannot understand, and listening to sermons on the worship of relics, or on prayer for the dead, or to the virgin Mary, the Sabbath would be almost a lost day. But when the pure truths of the Bible are taught, as in the United States, in the house of God, in the Sabbath-school, and in the family circle, the Sabbath is of inestimable value.

No nation could lose so much as ours by losing the Sabbath. It is the aqueduct which conveys the waters of salvation through our land, and none but an enemy to our liberty, as well as to our souls, will attempt to destroy it. If other nations, then, neglect the Sabbath, we should guard it as we guard our life. If other nations despise the Sabbath, we should esteem it as one of the choicest gifts of heaven to our country.

EVENING X.

MANNER OF KEEPING THE SABBATH.

Mrs. M. There are a few things more, my dear children, which I wish to say to you about the Sabbath, before we finish our conversations. I have shown you that God intended the Sabbath to be kept by all, in every age, and in every part of the world. I have shown you that it is very kind in God to sanctify the Sabbath for man, because the Sabbath is so well fitted for man's nature and condition. This evening I wish to converse with you *about* THE MANNER *in which the Sabbath ought to be kept.*

Let us see what the fourth commandment tells us about keeping the Sabbath. The first thing which it tells us to do, is to *remember* the Sabbath-day to keep it holy.

We must remember that it is the day which God has sanctified for himself, or we shall not be apt to keep it holy. We must not look at the Sabbath only as a day which it is expedient to keep, but as a day which God has commanded us to keep.

We must remember that the Sabbath was made for man, and that he needs it. We must not think it only a day which it may be well enough to keep but which may be neglected without any injury to the body, or to the mind, or to the welfare of the soul. We must remember how kind God is in giving us the Sabbath, when so many others do not know that there is any Sabbath.

We must remember how many are not permitted by their masters, or by those who employ them, to keep the Sabbath, while we may enjoy a day of holy rest.

We must remember that God requires us to keep the day holy. To keep it holy is to devote it to those purposes for which God has set it apart.

We must remember that God will require of us an account of our Sabbaths, and how we have kept them, and whether they have done us any good.

We must remember, above all, the great object of the Sabbath is to renew our souls, and fit them for God's service, and for an endless Sabbath above. For why is the Sabbath called the *Lord's day*, except that our Saviour arose on that day? Our Saviour from what? First of all, our Saviour from sin. And why was the Sabbath changed from the seventh to the first day of the week, if not because the Saviour arose on that day, having finished the work of redeeming man from sin and death? The light of every Sabbath should remind us that we are sinners, who need salvation through Christ Jesus. If we forget this, we shall not remember the Sabbath-day to keep it holy, as God designed.

We must remember, too, that the Sabbath furnishes special opportunities and means for securing the salvation of our souls. We must feel our need of salvation, and must use those means which the Sabbath offers, with a sincere desire to become the humble and faithful followers of Christ.

We must remember that our Sabbaths, in this world, will soon come to an end, and that we must use them as they are passing, or they will all quickly be gone, and our souls will be lost for ever.

We must remember how many Sabbaths we have misspent and wasted in sin; and show that we are penitent, by employing the present, and all future Sabbaths, in a better manner.

We must remember that these earthly Sabbaths are but a beginning of the eternal rest to all who do the will of God, and trust in the Lord Jesus Christ. We must think of the good, in every age, who have rejoiced in the earthly Sabbath, and are now rejoicing in the Sabbath of heaven. And we must remember that if we are christians, when another Sabbath returns to the earth, our souls may be joining in the songs of the redeemed before the throne of God. And we must remember—yes, my dear children, we must remember, that if we are not christians, if we have not repented of sin, if we have not trusted in Christ, if we have not made our peace with God, if we have not begun to be holy in heart, when our friends and neighbors, on another

Sabbath, shall meet in the house of prayer, we may be wailing among the lost spirits in the regions of eternal sorrow.

If we remember these things as we ought, we shall be likely to engage in a proper manner in the duties of God's holy day.

What then are these duties? The fourth commandment lays a foundation for them, by requiring *all to rest from their common labors.* The man who works with his hands during the other six days, must not work with his hands on the Sabbath. The man who works with his mind during the other six days, must not think on the same subject on the Sabbath. Whether labor is bodily or mental during the other six days of the week, it must cease on the Sabbath. "Six days shalt thou labor and do all thy work; but the seventh is the Sabbath of the Lord thy God; in it thou shalt not do any work." The first duty, on the Sabbath, is to rest from our common business.

But though the Sabbath requires men to rest from their common work, it does not require them to be idle and stupid. No, the Sabbath ought to be a busy day; that is, every part of it ought to be occupied with some duty which will make the heart better; some duty which falls in with the design of God in sanctifying the Sabbath.

George. May not people sometimes relax their minds on the Sabbath, mother?

Mrs. M. I do not suppose that every one ought to be thinking closely, or reading all the while on the Sabbath, when he is not engaged in the public or private worship of God, or in some similar duty. Some persons may be feeble, and need more relaxation on the Sabbath than others. They will do right if they take such relaxation as their ill health requires. But they ought always to remember, that the great object of the Sabbath is to sanctify their souls; and they should relax their bodies and their minds, only because they can, in this way, best accomplish the design of the Sabbath. Those who work hard and late on Saturday, because the Sabbath is coming, and they can then sleep, profane the day by such rest. They have no right to overwork their bodies on Saturday, and then try to recruit them on Sunday. It is robbing the soul, it is breaking the Sabbath, in the sight of God, as really as if they were at work. For it is taking a portion of the time which God has reserved for his own use, and employing it for our worldly purposes.

Another of the duties of the Sabbath *is social or public worship*. I have already told you that social worship is fitted to the nature and wants of man. It warms his affections when they grow cold, and quickens his zeal when it becomes faint and languid.

This was one of the duties required of the Jews on the Sabbath. "Six days shall work be done, but the seventh day is the Sabbath of rest, a holy convocation." (Lev. 23 : 3.) A holy convocation means a solemn assembly for the public worship of God. The heathen used to assemble and worship their idols. And men, at the present time, whenever they wish to show great honor to any day, meet and mingle their feelings together on that day. This is the reason why they assemble to celebrate the fourth of July, or the birth-day of Washington. They animate each other, by uniting in the celebration, and singing the same songs. I do not mention these examples, my children, for the sake of approving of every thing which is done on such occasions, but only to show that when men wish to manifest respect for any person, or for any day, they often assemble together, just as God commanded the Jews to meet and worship him on the Sabbath. Good men among the Jews loved to meet for social worship. They said, "How amiable are thy tabernacles, O Lord of Hosts! Blessed are they that dwell in thy house; they will be still praising thee. For a day in thy courts is better than a thousand; I had rather be a door-keeper in the house of my God, than to dwell in the tents of wickedness. My soul thirsteth for God, for the living God; when shall I come and appear before God? Then will I go unto the altar of God, unto God, my exceeding joy. O come, let us sing unto the Lord; let us make a joyful noise to the Rock of our salvation. Let us come before his presence with thanksgiving, and make a joyful noise unto him with psalms. O come, let us worship and bow down; let us kneel before the Lord our Maker. I was glad when they said unto me, let us go into the house of the Lord."

I suppose men who felt thus, would not wait for a command to go and worship God, any more than I should wait for a command to love George, and Charles, and Susan; or than an epicure would wait for a command to sit down at a table loaded with dainties. It was a privilege to David, and Asaph, and other holy men of that day, to worship God in his temple, and in the congregation of the righteous. If God would permit them to worship him in public, they would account it their "exceeding joy." I suppose a cloud, or a slight shower, would not have been thought excuse enough for not joining in the "holy convocation."

The Bible tells us that it was the "*custom*" of Jesus Christ, when on the earth, to attend public worship in the synagogue. And the apostles used to meet with their converts, and worship God on the Sabbath. They commanded men not to forget the "assembling of themselves together, as the manner of some" was, even so early. But men had more excuse at that time than we have for neglecting social worship. A person might lose his life if he met with the church of Christ, to worship God, and adore the Saviour. But notwithstanding the danger, Paul told those to whom he wrote, they must not forget to unite in social worship. The ancient christians would meet in tombs, and on board of ships, and in caves, and at midnight, rather than give up the privilege of social worship, even when they knew that they were watched, and if discovered, might be burnt at the stake, or be torn in pieces by wild beasts. I suppose one of these christians did not, on the morning of the Sabbath, think that if it was a little cold, or might be rainy, or he did not feel very well, he might be excused from social worship. The Holy Spirit has blessed social worship to the salvation of millions. Probably more have been brought to reflect on their ways, and to repent and turn to God, in consequence of public worship, than from any other cause. And at the present day very few become pious and humble christians who have lived in the neglect of public worship.

But for public worship, a large part of mankind would know very little of the doctrines of the Bible; for the name of God, and even the knowledge of God itself, would cease from the earth.

Good men still love the public worship of God. When sick, they long to be able to join in the prayers and praises of God's house, and they grieve that they cannot go with the multitude who keep holy day. And when health returns, they regard it as a delightful privilege to pay their vows unto the Lord, in the presence of all the people.

George. I remember that you read to us, the other evening, in the life of Mrs. Hannah More. She said the Sabbath was not only her day of rest, but her day of enjoyment—and that she went to church twice on the Sabbath.

Mrs. M. When you find a christian beginning to neglect public worship without any good reason, you may be almost sure that he is growing worldly. If he ever regains his christian feelings, he will be found in his place in the house of prayer. And while the tear of penitence flows down his cheeks, he will say in his heart, "I have gone astray like a lost sheep. Return unto thy rest, O my soul, for the Lord hath dealt bountifully with thee."

Public worship tends to make men feel how vain are the distinctions of rank, and wealth, and fashion. "The rich and the poor meet together," in the house of God. The worshipers have all one Father, and one Saviour. They have common sins to confess, and common wants to be supplied. They have similar temptations to overcome, and need the sanctifying influences of the same Spirit. All are bound to the same grave, and all the pious to the same heaven. The man of wealth is taught that however high his place is in the house of God, riches will not purchase him a seat at God's right hand. The man of learning is taught that holiness is accounted better than knowledge among the spirits of heaven. The fashionable and the gay are taught how much the robe of immortality outshines the brightest garments of earth.

But public worship will not be pleasing to God, or profitable to men, without some preparation. Before we go to church, we must pray for the blessing of God; we must read the Bible; we must feel that God is in his holy temple. The man who goes up to the sanctuary, thinking of his worldly business, his accounts, his clients, his crops, his ships, must not expect to hold communion with his Maker. Can the child, or the youth, expect a blessing, who goes to church, not to worship God, but to show a new dress, or see some companion or friend?

I have known children laugh and play, and be light-minded, during social worship. The blazing eye of God was fixed steadily on them, and I almost feared, every moment, they would be struck dead beneath his awful frown. I shudder when I see little children thoughtless and inattentive in the house of God. He is the same now as when he came down on Sinai in cloud and tempest, and he has told us that "holiness becometh his house for ever." And though fire does not break out and devour them, as it devoured Nadab and Abihu, still they cannot safely trifle with God's worship. He knoweth how, the Bible tells us, to reserve the wicked "unto the day of judgment, to be punished." It is painful to see these little children lifting up their puny hands, like hardened rebels, in bold defiance of their Maker.

People in the country sometimes live too far from church to return home between the morning and evening services. These often profane the Sabbath, by collecting into little groups, and talking about party politics and the news. The children and youth sometimes wander into the fields, or into the woods, and profane the Sabbath by gathering berries or nuts, or stealing fruit from gardens and orchards. Some wicked boy may usually be found among them, whose example and conversation will do more hurt in one hour than the labors of many christian mothers can repair during a week. If the Sabbath-school did nothing but keep children from profaning the Sabbath, between the morning and evening services, I have often thought this would be worth all the trouble and expense of sustaining it.

I think, however, that there is less playing and inattention among children, during public worship now, than there were many years ago. They have learned in the Sabbath-school to understand the minister better, and he often makes his sermons more simple and plain for the sake of the children.

Susan. I remember, mother, our minister said once, that when he saw children whispering or playing in meeting, he always thought they did not go to the Sabbath-school; for if they did, they would learn to fear God and respect his day and his house.

Charles. Is it any worse, mother, for children to play, than for their parents to sleep, during public worship?

Mrs. M. Children never have any excuse for playing in meeting, my son. But there is here and there a person who cannot keep awake, during the whole service, on the Sabbath. They have a disease, called the lethargy, which always makes them sleepy as soon as they sit down; no matter whether at home or abroad—whether they are alone or in company with their friends. Such persons I pity, for they cannot help being sleepy; and God will not mark it down against them as a sin, when they do all they can to keep awake.

There are others, however, whom God will not excuse for sleeping at church, while they ought to be engaged in his worship, or listening to his Gospel. Look, on some Sabbath, at a congregation of worshippers. There is a man leaning his head on the front of the slip. He is fast asleep. The minister is urging his hearers to awake to righteousness, for the end of their probation is at hand. But farmer Hughes is in a sound slumber, and does not hear a word.

George. Farmer Hughes is not a poor man, mother, and obliged to work hard.

Mrs. M. No, my son, he is one of the richest men in the town. He owns a great deal of land, and is continually buying more. But he tells people that he cannot keep awake at meeting, because he is in debt, and must work very hard during the week to pay for his land.

Yonder is another healthy-looking man mocking God and discouraging the minister, by sleeping during the sermon. That is Mr. Dickman, the blacksmith.

He has a fine set of customers, and is one of the most thriving men in the place. But he, too, is obliged, he says, to work so hard during the week, that he must stay at home and rest on the Sabbath if you will not excuse him for sleeping a little in the house of God.

Who is that changing his seat so often, to keep from drowsiness? That is Mr. Mortimer, the merchant. He is always sleepy when he eats a hearty dinner; and you must excuse him if he cannot help being drowsy on the Sabbath.

Charles. But I think, mother, that Mr. Mortimer, the merchant, had better eat a little less on the Sabbath than on other days, if he cannot keep awake at meeting.

Mrs. M. I think so too, Charles; but Mr. Mortimer thinks differently. He must always have a better dinner on the Sabbath than on other days— for he cannot attend to his business on that day, and so has leisure to see company. He makes his domestics stay away from church in the morning to prepare dinner for himself and friends—and then he is drowsy during the whole service, if he comes to church in the afternoon. But he does not come very often. I think if Mr. Mortimer knew he was to plead for his life, he would be careful not to eat so rich a dinner. And if he felt, as he ought, that he was to plead at church for the life of his soul, he would not compel his domestics to violate the Sabbath for the sake of getting him a dinner which only makes him drowsy and stupid.

It grieves me to think how plainly all these men show that they prefer their business to the worship of God; their bodies to their souls; and their money to salvation.

Self-examination is one of the duties to which we are invited by the Sabbath. This is a duty which cannot be neglected, safely, by any one, and there is no season so fit for it as the Sabbath. George, and Charles, and Susan need to spend a part of the Sabbath in self-examination, as well as their parents. They should examine their conduct for the past week, and see what they have done which is wrong; and then they should resolve to do better the week to come. Have they obeyed their parents cheerfully in every thing? Have they been kind to each other, not speaking a harsh word, or giving an unkind look, or indulging an unkind feeling?

How have they treated their playmates? Have they been proud and haughty towards them? Have they envied any of their playmates? Have they wanted any of their books, or pictures, or playthings? Have they obeyed all the rules at school, and tried to please their teachers, and to get their lessons well? Have they yielded to temptation to deceive, or to tell a falsehood? Have they wished to get above their classmates, and been sorry to have them do better than they? Have they neglected their duties to God? Have they omitted secret prayer and reading the Bible? These, and similar questions, children should ask themselves every Sabbath. And if they find they have failed in duty, as they certainly will find, if they examine their hearts and their conduct faithfully, they must be penitent for it before God, and pray for grace to avoid such sins in future.

All need to examine their hearts and lives, often and carefully; for without doing it, they will never know what are their faults, or what is their character, and their prospects for eternity. One of the greatest blessings of the Sabbath is, that it gives a season for attending to the necessary duty of self-examination.

EVENING XI.

MANNER OF KEEPING THE SABBATH.

Mrs. M. We will continue our conversation, this evening, about the MANNER of keeping the Sabbath.

Private devotion, reading and meditation make a part of the duties to be performed on the Sabbath. They ought, especially, to follow the worship of the sanctuary. It will do us little good to join in public prayer and praise, and hear a sermon, if we go home and converse about improper subjects. Some persons, when they return from church, converse about the dress worn by their neighbors, or what acquaintances they may have met, or what strangers they have seen. Others spend a good deal of time in criticising the sermon. It is too long, or too short; too practical, or too doctrinal; too plain, or too elegant. They are rarely just suited. This habit of finding fault destroys all the good which public worship might do them or the younger members of the family. It is a bad practice, and ought to be abandoned at once.

Much better would it be for them to go to their closets, as soon as they reach home, and pray that what they have heard may do them good; that they may not forget it; that it may fit them to perform duty, to bear trials, and to resist temptations during the week. If their minds are made serious by the public services, they ought to pray that their seriousness may continue; and if they have formed any good resolutions, that they may have grace to keep them.

Many persons would know little about the Bible if they had not leisure to study it on the Sabbath. Persons employed in factories, day-laborers and domestics, often cannot devote as much time to the study of the Bible as the good of their souls demands.

George. But do not these persons need to rest on the Sabbath?

Mrs. M. One end of the Sabbath is rest to the body and the mind, and we ought not, when we can avoid it, to get weary and fatigued on the Sabbath. But persons who work with their bodies during the week, can rest while they read the Bible and think upon serious things. A change of labor is sometimes a refreshment. A man who is tired of one kind of exercise, can often engage in another without feeling weary. It is a pleasure for one who has been hard at study all day, to cut wood, or walk, or ride on horseback. So a man who has been wearied by bodily labor can exercise his mind without fatigue. And God has so made the mind, that when men are weary by thinking of one kind of subject, they can often think of another without feeling weary. A distinguished judge in a neighboring state, used to study mathematics to refresh his mind when he had become weary with thinking about some difficult point of law.

There is a great variety in the duties of the Sabbath. Persons in health will not often be in danger of getting weary, if, when they are tired of one duty, they set about another.

I remember when most people had very few books to read on the Sabbath but the Bible. There were not many commentaries in the land, and there were among the common people no maps and books to explain the customs, and manners, and antiquities of the ancient nations, which are so often mentioned in the Bible. There was only here and there a religious biography, and there were no religious periodicals to give information about the kingdom of Christ. I suppose you wonder how we could contrive to make the Sabbath interesting and profitable.

It is strange that parents take so little pains to get books to aid their children in the study of the Bible. Scarcely any are so poor that they could not afford the trifling expense. When there were only a few books in the world, and those few were very dear, a learned man advised his friend to sell one of his eyes and buy a certain book, and read it with the other. Without any such sacrifice, parents might furnish their families with all the books necessary to explain the Bible.

Family instruction is another interesting duty on the Sabbath.

You may regard mankind as separated into three great divisions. One division is that of individuals. In this division every man stands by himself. The second division is that of families. This division includes several individuals who live together under the same roof. The third division is that of communities. This division is made up of a greater or less number of families living under the same government and laws.

The division into families was made in the garden of Eden, at the same time when God sanctified the Sabbath. The Sabbath is fitted to this division of men into families, and this division of men into families is fitted to the Sabbath. Like twin sisters, each aims to promote the welfare of the other.

It would be very strange, therefore, if when God gave the ten commandments, he had forgotten or overlooked this early division of mankind into families, which he had himself made. Nor did he forget or overlook it.

The first three commandments point out men's duties to God. The last five point out men's duties to the community in which they live. The fourth and fifth commandments point out, specially, men's duties as they live together in families. The fourth commandment, to be sure, includes social worship, and the fifth includes the obedience which men owe to rulers as well as parents. The fourth commandment has been fitly called a "*Family commandment.*" It mentions the parts of which families are composed more particularly than any other commandment of the ten.

Except in the hours of public worship, the bonds which bind families together into communities are dissolved on the Sabbath. It is as if the world was made up only of families, and there was no other society. The duties which men owe their families are very important and interesting. If children are not governed in the family, they will grow up restless and ungovernable. If they are wicked and irreligious in the family, they will be apt to continue wicked and irreligious all their days. I suppose that a large part of those who become pious, become so while they are children, and living under their father's roof. If the duties of the family are neglected, societies cannot be happy, and prosperous, and moral.

God has devoted a considerable portion of one day in seven to these important duties of the family. On other days the laborer is obliged to be absent from his family a great deal, and sometimes he must be absent the whole week. The mother is occupied with many cares, and cannot instruct her children so much as she wishes; and the children, too, are often either abroad at work, or at school, or too fond of play to attend to instruction. But the Sabbath comes. The poor man returns to his home. His family gather around him. The children, who were too playful to listen to what their mother told them, are now quiet and attentive. They see none of their companions on the green, trundling the hoop or knocking the ball. It is the hour for parental influence and counsel. Those who love the souls of their children will not let it pass unimproved. The father can now, without hurry or interruption, teach his children about their duties to God, their own souls, and to one another. While he sets them an example of devoting the Sabbath to religious duties, he can exhort, and, if necessary, command them to reverence God's holy day. He will teach them some good catechism, and explain it in a simple and cheerful manner. As evening approaches, he will call his family together, and read a sermon, or a chapter in the Bible. Then he will pray for a blessing on the public and private duties of the Sabbath, for the presence of God through all the unknown scenes of the coming week, and for a union, at last, with the redeemed, in the purer worship of the upper world.

The memory of my early Sabbaths is dear to me. But I remember no part of them with more interest and tenderness than the close of the day. When the shadows began to gather, a beloved father, now I trust among the just in heaven, would call us together, read a sermon, or a chapter in the Bible, and then offer a family prayer. I can remember, as if it were only yesterday, the very texts, and the very feelings of my conscience and my heart, as I listened to the pungent discourses of President Edwards, and others of a similar character. The recollection of these scenes often makes my spirit more tender than the most solemn truths which I now hear on the Sabbath. And even then, when my heart had been thoughtless during the worship of the house of God, these scenes in the family, which closed our Sabbath, would affect my mind too deeply to be forgotten through the whole week. When I think of my childhood, I cannot but feel that of all seasons for the instruction of children, the family circle, at the close of a Sabbath spent in the house of prayer, is the best. Let the scene be cheerful, but let it, too, be serious. Cheerfulness will make it pleasant at the time, and seriousness will fix it in the mind for many years to come.

God knew that many men would not love to keep the fourth commandment themselves, and that they would not be willing to let their children, and their domestics, and their beasts that labor, rest on the Sabbath. So God did not only say in the commandment, *men shall not work*, but *thou* shalt not do any work, thou, nor thy son, nor thy daughter.

Every parent is bound, not only to rest himself, but to let his children rest on the Sabbath. When they leave home to learn a trade, or to become clerks in stores, or to attend school, or to be domestics in families, he is bound to see that they have the privilege of keeping the Sabbath. And if he places them where they are not permitted to keep the Sabbath, he breaks the command as much as if he were to labor himself on his farm, or in his shop, during holy time.

Domestics have a claim to rest on the Sabbath, so far as is consistent with the comfort of a family. "Thou shalt not do any work, thou, nor thy son, nor thy daughter, nor thy man-servant, nor thy maid-servant." While resting themselves, and letting their children rest, men ought to be careful to see that their domestics not only have an opportunity to keep the Sabbath, but that they spend it in a proper manner. I would not keep a domestic from public worship a part of the day, as some do, for the sake of getting a warm dinner, and much less to prepare for company. And when some of the family must stay at home, it is wrong to make domestics stay more than their share. They ought to be willing to take their turn; but to make them do more than that is a violation of the fourth commandment.

"Thou shalt not do any work, *thou, nor thy cattle.*" The apostle asks, "Does God take care for oxen?" Yes, my children, he does, for his tender mercies are over all his works. Beasts that labor all the week need rest as well as man. And as the poor, patient ox had no voice to urge his claim, God wrote it down in the commandment, that oxen have a right to rest on the Sabbath. Beware how you deprive them of this right, for God takes the part of the weak against the oppressor. We may use horses to carry our families to public worship, and for similar purposes, which are consistent with the design of the Sabbath. But a merciful man will consider, whether it would not be well to let a horse rest, at some other time, which he employs a large part of the Sabbath for these necessary purposes. I remember hearing that a gentleman, on a visit to his friend, I think in Ireland, was surprised to see all the horses feeding in their stalls on Saturday. As this was quite unusual on other days, he inquired the reason. His friend told him that as they lived a long distance from church, he could not let his horses rest on the Sabbath, so he gave them the day of rest to which they had a right, on Saturday. He was a merciful man.

But let me remind you, my children, at the close of our long conversation on the manner of keeping the Sabbath, that *the duties I have mentioned must be performed in a proper spirit.* You may break the Sabbath while doing them all. If the heart and life are examined without a desire to grow better;

if the Bible is read only out of curiosity, or to see how many chapters may be read over in a day; if public worship is attended only from custom, or to see a friend, or because it is popular; if you pray and meditate only to quiet conscience, God will frown on your services, and a day will be lost, in which your soul might have been fitted for glory, honor, and immortality.

And without a proper spirit, the Sabbath will be as unpleasant as it is unprofitable. Its duties will be burdensome, and you will say in your heart, "When will the Sabbath be gone?" But if you have the spirit of the Sabbath in your soul, you will think its precious moments fly away too swiftly. You will almost wish to stop the sun in his course, as he descends towards the western mountains, and the shadows of evening begin to lengthen. You will feel with the poet, as you breathe the pure air, and enjoy the tranquil light of the Sabbath,

> Day of all the week the best,
> Emblem of eternal rest.

With such a spirit, the Sabbath will never be a weariness. We shall greet it with a cheerful welcome as it approaches; we shall spend it in joy and praise while it is passing, and when we must part, bid it an unwilling farewell.

You may repeat the hymn on *Sabbath Evening*, Charles, which I gave you last week to learn for the close of our conversation to-night.

CHARLES.

" Is there a time when moments flow
 " More peacefully than all beside ?
" It is of all the times below,
 " A Sabbath eve in summer tide.

" Oh then the setting sun smiles fair,
 " And all below, and all above,
" The different forms of nature wear
 " One universal garb of love.

" And then the peace that Jesus beams,
 " The life of grace, the death of sin,
" With nature's placid woods and streams,
 " Is peace without, and peace within.

" If heaven be ever felt below,
 " A scene so heavenly sure as this,
" May cause a heart on earth to know
 " Some foretaste of celestial bliss.

" Delightful hour! how soon will night
 " Spread her dark mantle o'er thy reign,
" And morrow's quick returning light,
 " Must call us to the world again.

" Yet will there dawn at last a day ;
 " A sun that never sets shall rise ;
" Night will not veil his ceaseless ray—
 " The heavenly Sabbath never dies."

EVENING XII.

VIOLATIONS OF THE SABBATH.

Mrs. M. I wish to converse with you a little while this evening, my dear children, *about* VIOLATIONS OF THE SABBATH.

George. How can we know, mother, when we do break the Sabbath? The commandment says we must not do any work, but you have told us that we may work some. You said domestics must not be made to work more on the Sabbath than is necessary for the comfort of the family. The commandment says that "cattle" must not work on the Sabbath, but you have told us it is right to make horses carry us to meeting. How do you know such things are right?

Mrs. M. Such things are allowed in the Bible. Our Saviour said his disciples had done right in plucking corn on the Sabbath when they were hungry. We conclude from this case that it is right to prepare food for the purpose of satisfying our hunger on the Sabbath, or to do other things necessary for our health and comfort. Our Saviour himself ate on the Sabbath, and from his example we conclude that we may do the same. But this does not authorize us to spend the day in feasting.

As to using our horses for carrying us to the

house of worship, we think the Bible justifies us in this too. The priests in the temple killed the lambs for sacrifice on the Sabbath. But our Saviour says they did not sin in doing this. It was a part of religious worship. If any of the other Jews had killed lambs on the Sabbath for their own use, it would have been a violation of the fourth commandment. We think that this example justifies us in doing, on the Sabbath, the labor which is necessary to prepare us for divine worship, and which cannot be done before the Sabbath comes. We think, too, it allows us to use our cattle for the same purpose, and that it is right, therefore, to employ them in carrying our families to the house of God.

I suppose every thing may be done that is *consistent with the design for which God sanctified the Sabbath*.

This design, as I have already told you, is that men should rest from their common business on the Sabbath, whether they labor with their bodies or with their minds. Beasts that labor are also to rest on the Sabbath. This rest for beasts can only be for their bodies, but for men there is a higher design. God means that men, while ceasing from labor, shall have leisure to refresh their minds, and improve their hearts by the public duties of his house, and the private duties of the family and the closet. He means that men shall become more serious, humble, heavenly-minded, devoted, and prayerful, by keeping the Sabbath. Every thing which falls in with this design of God in giving men the Sabbath, may be done on that day. And every thing which hinders this design must be avoided.

George. This rule would be enough to guide us in many cases, but there are some cases, I think, where we might still be in doubt.

Mrs. M. Well, then, my son, I will give you another rule. Avoid doing any thing on the Sabbath when you are doubtful whether it can be done without violating the fourth commandment. You will be safe in letting it alone, while to do it may be sinful.

The small-pox is infectious. If you go too near you will be very likely to catch it. I do not know just how near you can approach it and be safe. Suppose, now, you were passing in the neighborhood of a house where several persons are sick of the small-pox. And suppose you knew that if you kept ten rods distant you would be out of danger from the disease. Suppose, too, that you did not know but you might safely go within two rods—what would you do?

George. Why, mother, I do not wish to have the small-pox, and should be sure to keep at least ten rods from the house.

Mrs. M. Just so, George, you should do in regard

to violating the Sabbath. Some things it is very plain that you may do on the Sabbath. Some things it is quite as plain that you must not do. And about some other things, perhaps, there might be a little doubt. You should act in regard to these doubtful things just as you do about keeping at least ten rods from the house infected by the small-pox. You should entirely avoid them—then you will be sure of not breaking the fourth commandment.

I will show you what I mean, by some examples. It is doubtless right for you to ride to meeting from your home on the Sabbath. It is as clearly wrong, without any necessity, to travel on a journey upon the Sabbath. But a man who lives thirty miles off owes you a debt, and is about to fail. You may lose your debt if you wait till Monday. Perhaps you begin to ask yourself if it may not be right for you to get your horse and go and secure your debt on the Sabbath. It is a doubtful case, you say. If, then, you ask my advice, I counsel you not to venture too near the infected house. Keep at a safe distance. Better lose your debt than offend God by violating his command.

It would be clearly wrong for a man to leave his home, in Hartford, on Sabbath morning, and, without any other reason than to gain a day for business, go to New-York in a steam-boat. It would, I think, be as clearly right for him to go to New-York on the Sabbath, if his wife or his father was at the point of death, in the midst of strangers. But now, suppose he is in New-York, and does not wish to be absent from his family on the Sabbath. So he deliberates with himself whether he had not better take the steam-boat on the afternoon of Saturday, and reach Hartford early on the Sabbath morning, before meeting. If he were to ask my advice, I would say, do not venture yourself on board that boat. I think it is a manifest violation of the Sabbath. You may say you are in doubt. Run not the hazard, then, of violating the fourth commandment. You would not run the hazard of violating the sixth commandment, and becoming a murderer. Why run the hazard of becoming a Sabbath-breaker? Keep far off from the infected house.

Another man has a fine field of wheat. Just as the crop is ready for harvest it begins to rain. The rain continues several days. The wheat begins to sprout. The sun shines pleasantly on Sabbath morning, for the first time in several days. The man asks if he shall take his sickle and go into the field and reap the wheat, that his family may not suffer for want of bread.

George. I think, mother, that he might go, and not break the Sabbath.

Mrs. M. Plainly, it would not be right for him to work always on the Sabbath, even in harvest time. The Jews were commanded not to work on

VIOLATIONS OF THE SABBATH.

the Sabbath, even to gather in their crops. "Six days shalt thou work, but on the seventh day thou shalt rest; *in earing time and in harvest, thou shalt rest.*" It is as plain, I suppose, that if the man had gathered in his crop, and his barn was on fire, he might try, on the Sabbath, to put out the fire. But between these cases which are plain, comes the man with his field of damaged wheat. What shall we tell him? You, it seems, George, would tell him to go and gather his crop. I should not dare to tell him so. I fear his field would be too near the infected house to be safe reaping. In other words, the case is very doubtful, if not plainly wrong.

George. But the man says he is poor, and cannot afford to lose the crop.

Mrs. M. Yes, but if it is wrong, can he not afford to lose his crop as well as to offend his Maker, and perhaps lose his soul? Do you not remember what the prophet said when the king of Judah hesitated to obey the command to send away the mighty men of Israel, whom he had hired to fight for him, at the expense of a hundred talents of silver?

George. No, mother, I do not remember it. What did he say?

Mrs. M. Amaziah said to the prophet, "But what shall we do for the hundred talents which I have given to the army of Israel?" The prophet replied, "*The Lord is able to give thee much more than this.*" Amaziah thought he could not afford to obey God; but the prophet told him, God is abundantly able to reward those that make present sacrifices to obey his commands. God is able to give this poor man much more than his field of wheat, if he trusts God, and keeps the fourth commandment. Besides, what has the man's poverty to do with not obeying God? How rich must a man be to become under obligations to obey the ten commandments?

George. But, mother, would it be right for the man to let his wheat be spoiled? We ought not to be wasteful, and is it not a waste to let a fine crop of wheat be injured, so as to become unfit to eat? Why did God make the crop grow, if he did not mean to have the man reap it, and gather it into his barn?

Mrs. M. God may design that he shall gather it into his barn if he waits until Monday. Or God may have let the wheat grow so finely, to see whether the man would obey his commandment to keep the Sabbath day. It would not be so much of a waste to let the wheat rot on the ground, as to disobey God. Because the wheat has grown up, it is not certain that God ever intended it should be gathered. It is his wheat, and he will do with it as he pleases. How many times do the rains destroy crops, and the whirlwinds scatter them to the four quarters of heaven, and the lightnings consume them, after they are gathered into the barn? It is plain that God does not intend to have all the crops collected for the use of man and beast, which he causes to spring up and ripen. And no one can tell whether he has designed the crop of the poor man for this purpose. If God does not afford him a time for gathering his crop, it is plain that he never designed it should be gathered; and the poor man must be submissive, and trust God to provide for him and his family in some other way.

George. I think now, mother, that the poor man ought to let his crop alone on the Sabbath. It is at least doubtful whether he might properly gather it, and so on your principle he had better let it stand till Monday. But, mother, you said that if the crop was already gathered, and his barn should take fire on the Sabbath, he might try to put out the fire, and save his crop and his barn. Why might he do this any more than gather it into his barn, when it was in danger of spoiling?

Mrs. M. First, If the man were to put off gathering his grain, he does not know but it may be gathered just as well on the morrow. Cases have been known where a part of the people of a town gathered in their grain on the Sabbath, and it was injured, because it was damp, while the others, who waited until Monday, had fine weather, and gathered in their crops without injury. The chance is quite as good for securing the crop on Monday as on the Sabbath. At any rate, it may be as good, and so it is doubtful whether the work is necessary. But the case of the burning barn is different. If left to burn only a few minutes it will certainly be lost. It is necessary to put out the fire immediately, or it cannot be done at all.

Secondly, To gather in the crop of wheat will take nearly or quite all the day. But to put out the fire will take, probably, but a very little time. Dr. Dwight, who, on the one hand, was not bigoted, and, on the other, not lax, says, "That necessary work, which requires but a moment, may be lawful; when it would become unlawful if it required an hour."

Thirdly, It is more dangerous to allow that men may go into the field and work on the Sabbath, when it appears to be necessary, than that they may try to prevent the flames from consuming their houses or barns. For these fires occur very rarely, whereas harvest comes every year.

There is no difficulty in knowing when a fire is dangerous to a building, but it would be exceedingly difficult for an honest man always to judge when there was real danger of losing his crops, if he did not gather them on the Sabbath.

But it would be especially dangerous, because when men had once learned to labor on the Sabbath, even in doing what they think necessary, they would soon learn to labor for gain, without any pretence that it is necessary. In the case of fires there is no danger of this kind.

If you remember, my children, the two rules I have mentioned, you will not be in much danger of violating the Sabbath. What is agreeable to the design of God in sanctifying the Sabbath, you may do. But if you are doubtful whether any thing is agreeable to this design, let it alone.

Charles. When I spent a Sabbath with uncle John, a few months ago, he talked about politics almost all the while—was this right, mother?

Mrs. M. No, my son, I do not think it at all right. Try it by our rule. Would it make any one more heavenly-minded and prayerful to spend the Sabbath in talking about politics? Far from it.

We are tempted to break the Sabbath by improper conversation more than in almost any other way. We should not dare to work in a shop, or upon a farm, on the Sabbath—for we should think it very sinful. But while families are sitting together on the Sabbath, how common it is for some one to speak about the weather. Then another tells of some person who is sick, or has been hurt by accident. Another talks about some kind of business, or, perhaps, about the eloquence of some favorite preacher. A part of the family are pious, perhaps, and dislike such conversation; but they know how unwilling the rest are to hear any thing about religion, and so they join in violating the Sabbath. They ought to begin to talk on some serious subject, and if they cannot do that, to retire to some other room. The least they should do is to be silent. The Bible promises a blessing to those who do not speak their "own words" on the Sabbath. By their "own words," is meant words which are about worldly and improper subjects.

Susan. But, mother, if we do not talk about such subjects on the Sabbath, may we think about them in our hearts?

Mrs. M. No, my child, it is as wrong to think about worldly subjects on the Sabbath, as to talk about them. The Bible forbids us to find our "own pleasure" on the Sabbath—that is, to think about our business, or our amusements, or our plans for enjoyment. Susan broke the Sabbath to-day, when I overheard her telling Charles about the good things she should have to eat, and the fine clothes she should wear, when she went to keep thanksgiving with her aunt Mary.

Susan. I am sorry, mother, I thought about so foolish and wicked things on God's holy day.

Mrs. M. Ask God to forgive you, my child, and to make you more like those who keep the Sabbath in heaven.

George. Is it right, mother, to read histories and such books on the Sabbath?

Mrs. M. Try it by our rule. You once broke

the Sabbath by reading Hume's History of England, while your parents were at church. Did it make you any more serious, and prayerful, and heavenly-minded?

George. O no, mother. And I never mean to be so foolish and wicked again, for I could not say my prayers at night, I felt so guilty. But, mother, will you tell us what books we may read on the Sabbath?

Mrs. M. You can read the Bible, and religious biographies, and sermons, and the serious books which you get from the Sabbath-school library. There are hundreds and thousands of such books—but it would take too long to mention their names. When you are not acquainted with a book, you had better ask your father or mother, before you begin to read it, whether it is a proper book for the Sabbath. But if you cannot do that, remember the rules I have given you about keeping the Sabbath. A book is fit to be read on the Sabbath which makes the mind serious, and solemn, and devoted, and prayerful, and which falls in with the design of God in setting apart the day for his own service. This will very soon settle the question in most cases.

George. But there are some books which, when you try them by this rule, you will scarcely know whether they are fit for the Sabbath or not. What shall we do then?

Mrs. M. Then you must remember the other rule, not to do any thing on the Sabbath, the propriety of which you think is doubtful. Lay the book down, and do not touch or think of it again until the end of the Sabbath.

George. Is it right, mother, to go to the post-office on the Sabbath morning, as some of our neighbors do, and get their letters?

Mrs. M. People might just as well go out into the fields and work, or into their counting-rooms and post their books, as to take their letters out of the office on the Sabbath morning. If there was no other objection, it would be enough to show it is wrong, that it obliges the post-master, or his clerk, to do needless work on the Sabbath. But besides this, it makes those who get the letters "*think their own thoughts.*" Their letters are on business or on friendship, and generally make them more worldly, rather than serious, heavenly-minded, and prayerful.

George. But if one is expecting to hear from a sick friend, who needs his assistance, might he not go to the post-office then?

Mrs. M. If he could do his sick friend any good by getting the letter, which he could not do by waiting until the Sabbath closes, *then it would fall in with the design of the Sabbath* to get his letter Christ said it is right to help an ox or an ass out of the ditch on the Sabbath. So it is right to relieve pain and sickness on the Sabbath. It would not be right for a man to go out into the fields to look at his flocks of cattle and sheep, on the Sabbath, under the pretence of seeing whether an ox had not fallen into the ditch. So it is not right for a man to go to the post-office after letters of business, under the pretence of getting news about a sick or dying friend.

Men cannot, in such things, deceive God, and they do not very often deceive each other. The motive is so plain that a child may discover it.

George. But when a man is on a journey, mother, and puts up on Saturday night at a very noisy house, is it not right for him to travel the next day, if he can attend meeting on his way?

Mrs. M. No, my child. His horse has a right to rest on that day. And it is no excuse for travelling, that the house is noisy. He ought to stay and set the people a better example, and teach them not to violate the Sabbath. He has an opportunity to do good in this way—and he had better do it than sin against God by violating the Sabbath.

George. But is it not right, mother, for people to work on the Sabbath, if they have to get their support by their business, and their employers refuse to hire them unless they will work during holy time, when others are at rest? You remember when we were on our journey, last summer, in the State of New-York, a stage-driver said he did not like to work on the Sabbath. He said he could never go to meeting, and he did not love to live in this way. But he said that as the owners of the stages would have them run on the Sabbath, he might as well drive as any body else, for he must earn a living by working.

Mrs. M. I remember the man, and what he said. I pitied him, and I should not wish for the money which he earns for himself on the Sabbath, or for that which he earns for the stage-owner who hires him. It is the price of blood—not the blood of the body, but the blood of the soul. The man's excuse, however, was not a good one. He had better starve than live by violating one of the ten commandments every week. God can take care of the man if he puts his trust in him. God says in his word, "Trust in the Lord and do good, so shalt thou dwell in the land, and verily thou shalt be fed." And the excuse is good for nothing, that he might as well break the Sabbath as any one, since the Sabbath would be broken. He might as well say that he would kill the rich man, who is alone in the stage, and get his money; for if he does not kill the man and get the money, somebody else will. If somebody else will break the Sabbath, and make God angry, or commit murder and be hung for it, this is no reason why we should be so foolish and wicked.

Charles. But, mother, the government order the

stages to run, to carry the mail, on the Sabbath, and uncle John says they have a right to do this, if they please.

Mrs. M. Have the government a right to repeal the second commandment, and say men may be idolaters; or the third commandment, and say men may blaspheme the name of their Maker; or the sixth commandment, and say men may kill every body they meet?

Charles. O no, mother, that would be wicked enough. I think government would have no right to tell men they may do such things; and it would not be right for men to do so, if government told them they might.

Mrs. M. Where, then, did government get the right to repeal the fourth commandment, which says, " Thou shalt not do any work, thou, nor thy cattle ?"

Charles. I do not know, mother, and I do not think that uncle John could tell me.

Mrs. M. Government have no right to authorize men to violate the Sabbath, and men will find it no excuse hereafter, that government said they might trample upon the divine law. Governments are only men, and they will have enough sins of their own to answer for without bearing the sins of those they have encouraged to rebel against God.

Before closing our conversation, I will mention

a principle which learned men have taught, respecting works proper to be done on the Sabbath. It agrees with what I have told you this evening. I hope you will commit it to memory. "We may, on the Sabbath, do those works of charity and mercy which we could not do before the Sabbath, and which cannot be put off till the end of the Sabbath without showing a want of mercy and benevolence."

EVENING XIII.

MOTIVES FOR KEEPING THE SABBATH.

Mrs. M. We will converse to-night, my children, about the MOTIVES *which should lead us to keep the Sabbath.*

And, George, what is the best reason you can think of for doing any thing?

George. Why, mother, I can think of no better reason for doing any thing than *the command of God.* I suppose there can be no better reason for doing any thing, than that God commands it; or for not doing any thing, than that he forbids it.

Mrs. M. Then we have the best of all reasons for keeping the Sabbath holy; for we have seen, in these conversations, again and again, that God *commands* all men, wherever the Bible comes, to remember the Sabbath-day, and to rest from all their labor.

Can you think of any other reason, George, for keeping the Sabbath?

George. I do not think any other reason is necessary if men felt as they ought; but I suppose, if they can see that what God commands them is for their good, they may obey, sometimes, more cheerfully.

Mrs. M. It ought to be enough to make us do what God commands, that he commands it. We must believe it is right and proper, and for our good, whether we can see that it is so or not. But God is very kind and gracious, and many of his commands, he lets us see, are fitted to our nature and condition. This I have shown you is true of the fourth commandment. If God had not told us we must keep one day in seven, we ought to keep it *for our own good. Here, then, is another reason for keeping the Sabbath.*

When I tell you to go on an errand for me, Charles, do you think you ought to go because I command you?

Charles. Certainly I do think I ought to go, mother, because you love me so well, and because you do so much for me.

Mrs. M. And if I should tell you, Charles, that as you had been studying your geography and your Latin all the afternoon, the exercise would do you good, would this, too, be a reason why you should be willing to go on the errand for me?

Charles. Yes, mother.

Mrs. M. Now, Charles, if I were to promise you, that if you did the errand faithfully I would read to you an hour in the evening from some interesting book in your father's library, would that make you do your errand more quickly and faithfully?

Charles. I do not know that it ought, mother; but I should think you very kind in promising to reward me for doing what you had a right to make me do without any reward. And I love so well to sit down in the evening and hear you read history, that I should run all the way to the place to which you sent me, and back again.

Mrs. M. Then we have *another reason for keeping the Sabbath, for God promises to bless those who keep it as they ought.* "Blessed is the man that doeth this, and the son of man that layeth hold of it; that keepeth the Sabbath from polluting it." "If thou turn away thy foot from the Sabbath, from doing thy pleasure on my holy day, and call the Sabbath a delight, the holy of the Lord, honorable, and shall honor him, not doing thine own ways, nor finding thine own pleasure, nor speaking thine own words, then shalt thou delight thyself in the Lord; and I will cause thee to ride upon the high places of the earth, and feed thee with the heritage of Jacob thy father: for the mouth of the Lord hath spoken it."

If I should command Charles to do something which had often saved his life, he would be very foolish, and very ungrateful, and very wicked, if he refused to do it. *We have another reason, then, why we should keep the Sabbath, in what it has already done for our country.* Our forefathers were once heathen. They were heathen long since our Saviour came into the world, and the Sabbath was changed to the first day of the week. They would have been heathen still, had it not been for the Sabbath. This evening I might have been worshipping with you at the temple of some savage idol, or offering you as sacrifices to appease the anger of the gods. We can never be grateful enough for the gift of the Sabbath. The man who thinks it unnecessary, or burdensome, to rest one day in seven, almost deserves to be turned back to a state of heathenism, and groan under its yoke, until he learns his obligations to the Sabbath.

The liberty and the safety of our country depend upon the observation of the Sabbath, and this is a reason why we should observe it. I need only just mention this, for I have shown you, in former conversations, that no government, and especially no republican government, can last long without the Sabbath. One has well said, that, without the Sabbath our nation would be like a furious giant tearing in pieces himself, and every thing on which he could lay his hands.

Another reason why we should be very strict in keeping the Sabbath, at the present day, is *that many around us are indisposed to keep it.* It has been thought by some that our Puritan fathers were too strict, were gloomy, were superstitious, in their mode of keeping the Sabbath. But they would have had no Sabbath without a great deal of strictness. Others all around them used to spend the day in sports, in morris dances, and at the alehouse. Our ancestors would not join in such a violation of the Sabbath. They wanted that their example should reprove those who, in this way, profaned the Sabbath. And if our ancestors had not been so very strict in keeping the Sabbath, we should be spending our Sabbaths in sports and business.

Those who wish to recover the Sabbath from profanation must, at the present day, be even more strict than they would be at other times, instead of conforming to the wishes and example of the wicked.

The Sabbath, if not well kept, will be a curse to the country. This is another reason for observing it. There will long be a Sabbath of some kind in the land, whatever may be the character of the people. They would not, at once, labor on the Sabbath, even if they were to cease keeping the Sabbath holy. They would spend the day in gambling, in horse-racing, in drinking at the taverns, in fighting, and in riot. The shops would continue to be closed for some hours on the Sabbath. Factories would be shut; and the laborers not having to work, would spend the day in dissipation and sin. Our country must wither under the curse of such a Sabbath as this, if it will not spend the day in rest, and in the worship of God. There is no other choice. All our blessings, when we abuse them, become curses, and none more than the Sabbath. This is a reason why we should keep it holy unto the Lord.

The manner in which good men of other times observed the Sabbath, and their testimony respecting its benefits, is another reason why we should keep it holy. The good men in Israel loved and observed the Sabbath. The ninety-second psalm was written as a song for the Sabbath-day. Nehemiah would not suffer the men of Judah to labor on the Sabbath in treading wine-presses, or bringing in sheaves in harvest time, or in selling and buying food. Nor would he let the men of Tyre bring in fish or any kind of merchandise into Jerusalem on the Sabbath. He ordered the gates of the city to be shut " when it began to be dark before the Sabbath," and threatened to lay hands on the Tyrian merchants if they lodged without the walls on the Sabbath. The Lord Jesus Christ kept the Sabbath, with his disciples, when he was on the earth. The early Christians kept it as a day of sacred joy.

In modern times, good men have always loved and observed the Sabbath. Sir Matthew Hale, one of the greatest judges and best men that ever lived in England, urged his children to keep the Sabbath. He says, " I have found by experience, that the due observance of this day, and the duties of it, have been of singular comfort and advantage to me, and I doubt not that you, my children, will find it so to you. I have found, by a strict and diligent observation, that a due observance of this day hath ever joined to it a blessing upon the rest of my time; and the week that hath so begun, hath been blessed and prosperous to me; and on the contrary, when I have been negligent of the duties of this day, the rest of the week hath been unsuccessful and unhappy to my secular employments. And this I do not say slightly, but upon a long and sound observation and experience."

The celebrated Dr. Johnson, the author of the Rambler, and of many other books, was one of the greatest scholars in the world. He was very strict in keeping the Sabbath. A lady once asked Dr. Johnson if he did not think the Dean of Derry a very agreeable man. He made her no answer.

She repeated the question. "Child," said he, "I will not speak in favor of a Sabbath-breaker to please you or any one else."

When Dr. Johnson was on his death-bed, he sent for Sir Joshua Reynolds, a very celebrated painter. After talking with him seriously for a long time, Johnson told Sir Joshua that he had three favors to ask of him, and he hoped he would not refuse a dying friend. Sir Joshua said he would not refuse. The first request was, "that he would never paint on a Sunday;" and the third, that he would read the Bible whenever he had opportunity, and that he would never omit it on the Sabbath.

When the late Dr. Porteus, bishop of London, was sick of the disease of which he died, he heard a report that a club, or company of men, had agreed to hold meetings on the Sabbath. This was not for worshipping, but for mirth and enjoyment. The Prince of Wales, afterwards George the Fourth, king of Great Britain, was at the head of this club. The good bishop was much grieved at the report, and requested to see the prince. The request was granted, and the day for the visit appointed. The bishop was supported by two servants, and hardly able to move with their assistance. When he got to the apartment of the prince, he begged him to fix on some other day for the meeting of the club. The prince treated him very kindly, and seemed much affected. The prince said that the club was meant for charitable purposes, but if the day of the meeting could be changed to Saturday, it should.

How often does Henry Martyn, the refined scholar and the lovely christian, speak of the Sabbath! How often he mentions its delights. On one occasion he writes, "Passed this Lord's day with great comfort and precious solemnity of soul. Glory to God for his grace. Reading the Scriptures and prayer took up the first part of the day Almost every chapter I read was blessed to my soul. I felt as if I could never be tired of prayer."

You will find the same love of the Sabbath in the memoir of David Brainerd. Indeed, eminent christians could not live without the Sabbath.

With the examples of such men, my children, on your side, you never need be ashamed to keep the Sabbath, wherever you may be. Dare to be singular, if it is necessary for you ever to be in the company of those who break the Sabbath. Let them ridicule your bigotry, as they may call it. I had rather you would be called bigots, for following the example of such men, than that you should be praised for breaking the Sabbath.

One who keeps the Sabbath, can do much more good to others, than if he neglects the Sabbath. This is a reason why every person who wishes to be useful should observe the Sabbath strictly. It is not great talents so much as great piety, which makes men useful. It is not so much a clear and strong intellect, as a warm, and affectionate, and humble heart. I suppose there have been a great many men in our country who knew more than David Brainerd and Samuel J. Mills, a great many men of much finer talents than they. But few men in our country have been so useful. And the reason is, that few men in our country have been so pious But a man who disregards the Sabbath will never be an eminent christian. If we would be useful to others, then, we must keep the Sabbath holy unto the Lord.

The Sabbath, too, is a sign of our reverence for God, a visible sign which all can easily understand. While others go on with their business or their pleasures, the man who keeps the Sabbath stops one day in seven. Why does he break off his labors and his amusements? God has commanded him to "remember the Sabbath-day to keep it holy." It is a visible mark of his reverence for the authority of God, and a reproof to all who set at naught this authority. Men respect others for keeping the Sabbath as God's day, just as they respect one who, in the midst of the profane and unprincipled, is not afraid to lift up his voice and say, "Thou shalt not take the name of the Lord thy God in vain; for the Lord will not hold him guiltless who taketh his name in vain."

One might as well expect to convince others

that he fears God, when he every day blasphemes or trifles with his name, as expect to convince them that he at heart fears God, when he violates the Sabbath. The man who breaks the Sabbath himself, respects others who keep it more than he does those who break it. And if he ever needs to intrust the care of a child, or the care of money to others, he will intrust them sooner to those who keep, than to those who break the Sabbath.

I have no doubt the late Mr. Wilberforce was much more useful for his regard to the Sabbath. He would not attend to business on the Sabbath even to please the highest lord in the land. All felt that he was sincere in his religion; and they loved and respected Wilberforce, even while they would not love and respect the God whom Wilberforce adored, and the Saviour in whom Wilberforce trusted.

No lady in England, perhaps, was ever loved and respected by the great and fashionable so much as Mrs. Hannah More. But she was a strict observer of the Sabbath. When she was among the fashionable and the refined; among statesmen and men of wealth, who disregarded the Sabbath, she would still keep it holy. This was a constant memorial to her friends and acquaintances that she reverenced God. It was a constant testimony against their violations of the Sabbath, and neglect of the service of their Maker. She was once spending some time on a visit to a friend. A fashionable circle were visiting the same family. Some one proposed, on the Sabbath, to have music. She began to feel uneasy, when Garrick, the celebrated actor, who was one of the visiters, turned round and said, "Nine," that was the name he generally gave her, "you are a *Sunday woman;* retire to your room, I will recall you when the music is over." Her regard for the Sabbath gave her much power over the minds of the gay, the wealthy, and the noble.

The Sabbath is the great moving power of the moral world, and this is a reason why we should regard it, and keep it holy. I will explain what I mean when I say the Sabbath is the great moving power of the moral world. You remember that on our journey last summer we stopped at a manufacturing village, and visited several large factories, which stood near each other, on the same stream. There were a great many wheels moving very rapidly. Every thing seemed busy and almost alive. It was a very curious sight. Susan was quite astonished, and wanted to know what moved the first wheel. One of the workmen showed her how it was moved by another wheel. Then she wanted to know what moved the second wheel; and he showed her how it was moved by another wheel. And then she wanted to know what moved the third, and the fourth, and so on. There were a great many wheels, I do not know how many, one moving another. At last she wanted to know what set them all in motion, and kept them moving. So the workman showed her a great wheel, against which the water from the pond pressed; and he told her that this wheel moved all the rest, and was itself set in motion by the water from the pond. The water from the pond, he said, was the great moving power.

So, my children, in God's government over men, there are, I may say, many wheels. One wheel moves another, and that wheel moves another, and so on, through a great number. The works of God, the providence of God, the Bible, prayer, religious meditation, and all the means of grace, are only, I may call them, so many wheels set in motion to make the heart better. But without the Sabbath, these wheels would stand still. It is the Sabbath which sets them in motion, and keeps them moving, so as to improve the heart. The Sabbath is necessary to the success of all the means which God uses for the sanctification of men. It is the great moving power of the moral world, without which all the wheels and all the machinery which human, and I might almost say, divine skill could contrive to govern and sanctify men, would be of no use. We ought, then, to be very careful to keep the Sabbath; for without it, whatever else we do, for the spiritual benefit of ourselves or others, will be almost in vain.

I will mention out one more reason why we should observe the Sabbath. It is *the different ends to which a well kept, and an abused Sabbath lead in the future world.* We must render an account for our Sabbaths at last, before the bar of God. You would shudder if you were guilty of one breach of the sixth commandment, and were to be tried for murder in the court of heaven. How much more would you shudder if you had been guilty of murder *every week*, from your childhood until the end of your life. But he that said, "Thou shalt not kill," said, also, "Remember the Sabbath-day to keep it holy." And you disregard his authority no more by committing murder, than by breaking the Sabbath.

The blessing of God on a well kept Sabbath will prepare you for his presence, and the smiles of your Saviour, and the company of angels and all the good that will have gone from this world to heaven. There you will enjoy, for ever, the rest which remaineth for the people of God. There

> Storms of sorrow never blow,
> Temptations never come.

There

> Joy like morning dew distils,
> And all the air is love.

But abuse your Sabbaths, spend them in labor, in amusements, in visiting, or in idleness, and you sink to that world of darkness and gloom, where there is "no peace to the wicked," and where the weary are never at rest.

EVENING XIV.

DANGERS THREATENING THE SABBATH.

Mrs. M. This evening, my children, we must close our conversations about the Sabbath. I have only a few things more to say to you on the subject. When Charles and Susan return from their visit of two or three weeks to their aunt Mary, if our lives are all spared, perhaps we will converse about some other subjects for a few evenings.

Susan. I love to spend Thanksgiving with aunt Mary, and I love to play with cousin Jane and cousin Edward, but I think I shall love to come back and see my dear mother, and hear her talk again, on Sabbath evenings.

Mrs. M. The existence of good institutions in the United States, my children, depends, as I have told you, almost entirely on the manner in which the Sabbath shall be kept. With the Sabbath they will prosper, without it they are ruined. Will the

Sabbath, then, continue to be observed, as in past years, in this country? *Will it be not merely a day devoted in part to public worship, and in part to amusement, and in part to business, but a day of holy rest, such as was kept by our forefathers?*

WHAT ARE THE THINGS FROM WHICH WE HAVE REASON TO FEAR THAT THE PEOPLE OF OUR COUNTRY WILL GROW MORE AND MORE CARELESS ABOUT OBSERVING THE SABBATH?

This is what we will converse about this evening. It concerns us all, my children, but it concerns you, probably, more than your mother. The tall grass will soon be growing over my grave, and the strifes and tumults above my head will not disturb my sweet repose. But you are young, and hope to see many years. How will the Sabbath be regarded in our country half a century hence, is a question more interesting to each of you than you can easily imagine, or I express.

We have reason, then, to fear that the people of our country will more and more disregard the Sabbath, *from the transportation of the mail on that day.*

I have heard it stated that thirty thousand persons violate every Sabbath on account of the transportation of the mail. This includes not only the mail-carriers, but post-masters and their clerks, tavern keepers, stage proprietors, and a multitude of others. I do not doubt that the number is quite as great as it has been stated, if we include those who travel in the stages with the mail. But this is only a small part of the evil. A great many people are encouraged by the example of the government to travel in their own carriages. They think, or try to think, that what the government sanctions cannot be wrong. The sacredness of the Sabbath is destroyed, in the minds of thousands, by this act of the government, and they cease to regard the fourth commandment as binding, and the Sabbath as holy.

Whether the prayers and efforts of good people can raise the Sabbath from the dust, when it is trampled down every week by the order of government, is quite uncertain.

Another reason for fear that the Sabbath will be less regarded in the United States, *is the growth of large cities*. They extend their influence farther and farther into the country, as they increase in size and wealth. Many go to these cities on business, others for pleasure and curiosity. They see the Sabbath violated by the wealthy and the gay, and when they return home, they think it unfashionable to observe the Sabbath.

These cities send out their steam-boats, and their sail-boats, and their parties of pleasure to all the country around. Thousands thus profane the Sabbath by sailing and riding, and they make other thousands violate the Sabbath in providing for their wants; while multitudes learn to imitate their bad example. The more canals, and rail-roads, and steam-boats connect the large cities with the country, the more rapid, I fear, will be the increase of Sabbath-breaking.

Another reason for fear that the Sabbath will be more and more disregarded, *is the increase of manufacturing villages*. The population of these villages is composed, chiefly, of young men and women. They will be apt to feel that there is no great harm in walking and riding a little on the Sabbath, when they are shut up so much the rest of the week. Many of them have been taught by pious parents at home to keep the Sabbath. These will be in danger of yielding to the arguments, or invitations, or examples of their companions.

Thus the whole region round may find the quiet of the Sabbath disturbed by parties of pleasure from a manufacturing village. I know that many of these villages are among the most moral and orderly parts of the country, and that all might become so. But it cannot be done without more pains than we can expect will always be taken.

Another reason for fear that the Sabbath will cease to be kept strictly in our country, *is the increase of luxury and wealth*. The taste for traveling, and for visiting fashionable places, such as Ballston, and Saratoga, and the Virginia Springs, the Falls of Niagara, and the White Mountains, will increase with the increase of luxury and wealth. When people are absent from home, and especially on a journey, they are prone to violate the Sabbath. In some parts of our country, I am told that about as many stages run on the great routes on the Sabbath, as on any other day, and they are as well filled with passengers. This increase of traveling threatens to trample the Sabbath in the dust.

The increase of luxury and wealth will tempt many to indulge in entertainments, and dinner parties, and other things of a similar kind, which will unfit them for the Sabbath, and break the rest of their domestics. The example will extend from one circle to another, and we cannot set any bounds to the evil. The violation of the Sabbath by the nobility and the wealthy in England, is one of the principal causes of the violation of the Sabbath by the lower classes.

The growing want of religious instruction offers another reason for fear that the Sabbath will be more and more profaned in our country. A congregation of more than one thousand is added to our population every day. I fear that many of these will be destitute of the means of religious instruction, until they have no regard for holy time.

The circumstances of the people in the new settlements are unfavorable to keeping the Sabbath. They want to clear their land, and build a log-house to live in, when they first settle down in the forests. They feel that they may work on the Sabbath, to get a house to shelter them, and a little land clear for corn to feed their families. And it is hard to begin to keep the Sabbath again, when they have once formed the habit of breaking it. Many of the people, however, had not kept the Sabbath in their former abode. Some of them came from Europe, and some of them from places in this country where the Sabbath is disregarded. The woods will echo on the Sabbath to the sound of the axe, or to the gun of the hunter, but not to the voice of prayer and praise. There is no meeting for the worship of God, and for hearing the invitations of his mercy. The people rove about in the fields, and spend the day in idleness, if they do not spend it in labor.

I fear, too, that *there is an increasing number of persons in our land who dislike all religious restraint. These will hate the Sabbath, and try to destroy it.* They will call it superstition to rest on the Sabbath, and devote the day to the service of God, and the welfare of our own souls. They will laugh at those who observe the Sabbath, and call them old fashioned and bigoted. They will claim to be more liberal and enlightened than their neighbors, and to be less gloomy and fanatical than their Puritan fathers. If you will let them ride, or walk, or visit, as much as they please on the Sabbath,—or travel when they are on a journey,—

or post their accounts now and then at home,— or work on their farms whenever they choose to think it is necessary, they will have no objection to such a Sabbath. But they will cast off a Sabbath which restrains them from pleasure or sin.

But what is more discouraging still, even good people, in different parts of the world, appear to be growing lax in keeping the Sabbath.

A hundred years ago the Sabbath was much better kept in Europe, and in this country, than it is now. Formerly, in Scotland, officers went round in different quarters of the large towns, during public worship, to see if any persons were absent from church without a good excuse. A writer says of Scotland in 1763, "It was fashionable to go to church, and people were interested in religion. Sunday was strictly observed, by all ranks, as a day of devotion, and it was disgraceful to be seen in the streets during the time of public worship." The same writer says, that in 1783, or twenty years afterwards, "Sunday was by many made a day of relaxation, and young people were allowed to stroll about at all hours."

This was a great change. But a similar change appears to have been going on in England. In 1761, an ambassador was obliged to put off his journey to Monday, "*because he could get no wagoner to carry goods on a Sunday.*"

In New England the people were, at that time,

equally strict in keeping the Sabbath. But about the same period in which the change took place in England and Scotland, there was a change in this country. The old French war, and after that the war of the American revolution, turned off the thoughts of the people from religious subjects. They no longer kept the Sabbath as it was kept by our forefathers. The revolution in France increased the evil. For forty or fifty years, in Europe and America, good people seem to have been growing more and more negligent in keeping the Sabbath, though it is said that the higher ranks in Great Britain are beginning to observe it more strictly. I hope it is so, and that their example may be imitated in our own country.

The increase of canals, and rail-roads, and steamboats, and similar means of rapid traveling, is unfavorable to the strict observance of the Sabbath. Boats pass one place on the Great Western Canal, in the State of New-York, at the rate of one in every fifteen minutes on the Sabbath, as well as on other days. It is difficult to stop men and make them rest one day in seven, when they are eager in pursuing their business or their pleasure. The faster they can travel, the more of a hardship they seem to consider it to be checked by the Sabbath. The more they need the Sabbath to calm their excited minds, and recruit their exhausted bodies, the less they are grateful for the privilege of rest.

Roman Catholics in Europe are sending over money and men to extend their religion in the United States. *If they should succeed, and their religion should spread over the land, the Sabbath would be ruined.* Roman Catholics never keep the Sabbath as it is kept by Protestants. In Spain, the Sabbath is a day for the cruel amusements of bull-baiting and cock-fighting.

In Paris, "the shops are generally open; the markets are thronged as on other days; carts, and drays, and all sorts of vehicles designed for transportation of merchandise are in motion; buying and selling, and manual labor proceed as usual: there is rest neither for man nor beast. In the afternoon the shops are generally closed; labor is suspended, and the remainder of the day is devoted to pleasure. It is their gayest holiday." Another traveler says, that were a New Englander to arrive at Malta on the Sabbath, "he would not know that it is Sunday. A few shops are closed, but the doors of a vast many more are spread wide, and their windows are stuffed full as usual. The poorer people are going about the streets crying wares, water, and fruit for sale. The market is supplied with fish, flesh, and garden stuffs, and is frequented by purchasers as on other days. Children are playing abroad. Porters in their daily apparel wait at the corners of the streets to take burdens, or other commissions which may offer, and watermen are plying their skiffs in the harbor and inlets." We may learn from these descriptions how the Sabbath would be spent in the United States if the Roman Catholic religion should prevail here.

In New Orleans, where the larger part of the people are Roman Catholics, the Sabbath is greatly profaned. Amusements and business are common. Only a short time ago, a Roman Catholic cathedral was consecrated on Sunday in St. Louis, the capital of Missouri. Several military companies, both horse and foot, fully armed and equipped, were on parade, from six o'clock in the morning until four o'clock in the afternoon. There was all the appearance of a military review. A band of music belonging to the United States' army was present, and the sound of fifes, and drums, and clarionets, and bassoons, was mingled with the shouts of the rabble and the roaring of cannon. The cannon were placed immediately in front of the cathedral. The soldiers were furnished with food and wine, and were complimented for their attendance in the sermon at the consecration. *All this parade was got up by the Roman Catholic bishop of St. Louis; and three or four bishops, and about thirty ecclesiastics were present.* So you see what sort of Sabbaths we should have if popery were to prevail in our country.

I might mention some other things which make

me fear that the people of our country will become less and less strict in keeping the Sabbath, until at last they will cease to feel that it was sanctified by God, and must be spent in his service.

George. Is there no way, mother, in which the Sabbath can be preserved to our country?

Mrs. M. If good men could feel there is danger that the Sabbath will be lost, and unite in its defence, something might yet be done. But good men are often so engrossed with other things, that they do not seem to see the dangers which threaten the Sabbath. While they are contending about trifles, I am afraid the enemies of religion will strike a fatal blow at the Sabbath, and destroy all that is holy and excellent in the land.

George. If *men* will not do any thing to save the Sabbath, is there nothing, mother, which *children and youth can do?*

Mrs. M. Yes; children and youth can pray that the Sabbath may not be taken from our land, lest we should be smitten with a curse, and the God of our fathers should leave our nation to ruin. On the children and youth who are now growing up, will rest the responsibility of deciding whether the Sabbath shall be only a day of sport and amusement—or whether it shall be a day when the poor shall rest and be refreshed, and when souls shall be sanctified, and fitted for heaven. You, my children, and those of your age, will decide whether the Sabbath in this country shall be a day, in which God will delight to bless his people; or a day, for the abuse of which, he will inflict on our land the severest judgments.

For this reason, I have tried to show you the value of the Sabbath, and your obligations to keep it. The struggle to preserve the Sabbath, you see, from what I have told you this evening, will be hard; but remember, my children, that your mother commands you to surrender every thing else sooner than the Sabbath. Give up property, give up honor, give up life—but never, no, never give up the Sabbath. Go sooner to the stake; sooner let the earth drink your blood, than yield up the Sabbath, which you have received, as a precious legacy, from your pilgrim fathers. *Remember that to Americans a well kept Sabbath is a badge of liberty. Without it, they can never be free. With it, they can never be enslaved.* It is written in the counsels of heaven—it is written in the experience of other ages—it is written on the tomb-stone of disobedient nations, "REMEMBER THE SABBATH DAY TO KEEP IT HOLY, OR PERISH UNDER THE WRATH OF AN INSULTED GOD."

THE END.

SGCB Titles for the Young

Solid Ground Christian Books is honored to be able to offer a full dozen uncovered treasure for children and young people.

The Child's Book on the Fall by Thomas H. Gallaudet is a simple and practical exposition of the Fall of man into sin, and his only hope of salvation.

Repentance & Faith: *Explained and Illustrated for the Young* by Charles Walker, is a two in one book introducing children to the difference between true and false faith and repentance.

The Child at Home by John S.C. Abbott is the sequel to his popular book *The Mother at Home*. A must read for children and their parents.

My Brother's Keeper: *Letters to a Younger Brother* by J.W. Alexander contains the actual letters Alexander sent to his ten year old brother.

The Scripture Guide by J.W. Alexander is filled with page after page of information on getting the most from our Bibles. Invaluable!

Feed My Lambs: *Lectures to Children* by John Todd is drawn from actual sermons preached in Philadelphia, PA and Pittsfield, MA to the children of the church, one Sunday each month. A pure gold-mine of instruction.

Heroes of the Reformation by Richard Newton is a unique volume that introduces children and young people to the leading figures and incidents of the Reformation. Spurgeon called him, *"The Prince of preachers to the young."*

Heroes of the Early Church by Richard Newton is the sequel to the above-named volume. The very last book Newton wrote introduces all the leading figures of the early church with lessons to be learned from each figure.

The King's Highway: *Ten Commandments to the Young* by Richard Newton is a volume of Newton's sermons to children. Highly recommended!

The Life of Jesus Christ for the Young by Richard Newton is a double volume set that traces the Gospel from Genesis 3:15 to the Ascension of our Lord and the outpouring of His Spirit on the Day of Pentecost. Excellent!

The Young Lady's Guide by Harvey Newcomb will speak directly to the heart of the young women who desire to serve Christ with all their being.

The Chief End of Man by John Hall is an exposition and application of the first question of the Westminster Shorter Catechism. Full of rich illustrations.

Call us Toll Free at 1-877-666-9469
Send us an e-mail at sgcb@charter.net
Visit us on line at solid-ground-books.com

www.ingramcontent.com/pod-product-compliance
Lightning Source LLC
Chambersburg PA
CBHW032112090426
42743CB00007B/328